MW01235625

The

Jesus Mood

Discovering the Treasure
of Imperative Faith

Richard K. Murray

Outskirts Press, Inc.
Denver, Colorado

The Jesus Mood
Discovering the Treasure of Imperative Faith
All Rights Reserved.
Copyright © 2009 Richard K. Murray
V4.0

Outskirts Press, Inc.
http://www.outskirtspress.com

ISBN: 978-1-4327-2334-7

Library of Congress Control Number: 2009924410

Outskirts Press and the "OP" logo are trademarks belonging to Outskirts Press, Inc.

PRINTED IN THE UNITED STATES OF AMERICA

Directed by Sarah Murray

Thanks Sandy V. and Marie for all your help and input

Table of Contents

Introduction

Are you tired of being tired? Frustrated about being frustrated? Angry about being angry? Hopeless about being hopeless? If so, this book was written for you. The cure for every foul mood is *The Jesus Mood* - - the total cure, the perfect cure.

Bad moods. Sad moods. Weak moods. Bleak moods. Poor moods. Bored moods. Dark moods. Stark moods. Mood altering. Mood faltering. "I AM NOT IN THE MOOD!" has become the motto of fallen man. The word "mood" has been hijacked by hopeless hearts to describe our various forms of misery, boredom, madness and unbelief.

Jesus is here to rescue and redeem the word "mood." Mood is about to become a rainbow label of many glorious colors. Light moods. Bright moods. Sure moods. Pure moods. Strong moods. Song moods. *The Jesus Mood* replaces all man-made moods of failure with His God-made mood of faith.

Jesus is always in the mood for love - - always. God is love. Jesus is God. Individually, we are God's children. Corporately, we are Christ's bride. God so loved us He gave us the life, death and resurrection of Jesus. When we take communion, we not only are to remember Jesus' sacrifice, but we are also to remember to continually partake of Jesus' divine nature which indwells us (2 Pet. 1:3-4). Jesus' divine nature includes His mood of constant joy, appreciation, confidence and hope. Jesus was always in the mood for love because He always cleaved to the nearness of His Heavenly Father. As we cleave to the nearness of our indwelling Jesus, we too can always be in the mood for divine love - - simply because we are near Him.

When it comes right down to it, your mood is the most practical and basic thing you can offer to God. Mood includes focus, desire, willingness, confidence, availability and energy. To be in the mood for something requires focus <u>on</u> it, desire <u>for</u> it, willingness <u>toward</u> it, confidence <u>about</u> it, availability <u>to</u> it and energy <u>in</u> it. Jesus continually offered His mood to the Father at all times and in all places. This is why Jesus perfectly reflected the nature and authority of God. This book is about renewing our each and every mood in Christ. The importance of our mood cannot be overstated.

Mood is everything. As your mood, so are you. Your mood is your "mode of being" - - your current overall heart posture - - the absolute fuel gauge of your faith's fervency in God "now," this very moment. Your mood is the thermometer that reveals your current passion levels for life. A good mood reveals high and healthy levels of energy, hope, patience and confidence. A bad mood exposes high and unhealthy levels of anger, frustration, dread and sadness.

We don't relate to our children because we are "not in the mood." We don't open ourselves wholeheartedly to our spouses because we are "not in the mood." We don't smile, laugh and rejoice about life because we are "not in the mood." Work is burdensome and oppressive because we are not "in the mood." We don't spend time in prayer or the Scriptures because we are "not in the mood." We don't minister the life of Christ to the lost world because we are "not in the mood."

Trillions of dollars are spent annually on "mood-altering" events involving drugs, entertainment and sports. They work - - but only temporarily. The crash comes. The bad mood returns worse than before. The roller coaster of up and down. The revolving doors of in and out. The treadmill of over and over. The insecurity and instability of our mood slowly gnaws all our confidence away.

Why can't we stay in a good mood? Death, depression and darkness are relentless bounty hunters always on our trail armed to the teeth with bad words, bad thoughts and bad feelings. The end result is a tormented existence where joy, confidence and courage come and go, mostly "going" the older we get. Kierkegaard said we begin this life yawning and end up screaming. We let our fears define us, our failures condemn us and our insecurities rule us. It seems that the only options are to give up, numb up or dumb up. Many give up by becoming miserable and hopeless people. Many numb up by endlessly medicating themselves with drugs or entertainment which either deaden or artificially stimulate their feelings. Still, many others dumb up by just not caring. These poor souls lead shallow lives in which they never hunger for anything deeper, better or truer.

However, I have some wonderful news! There is a way out of bad moods - - forever. There is a way to consistently abide in ever-increasing good moods. No more doubt. No more insecurity. No more fear. Are you in the mood for this news? If you are in the mood for it, I promise you will get the mood of it - - this is *The Jesus Mood*. There is only one thing you must give up to obtain this mood and one thing only - - you must give up uncertainty toward God. Feel free to be uncertain toward everybody and everything - - except God. He must become the sole object of all your certainty. Then and only then will your mood be constant, steadfast and immovable, abounding in all joy and peace in believing.

Our greatest obstacle is "shoulder-shrugging" Christianity which can only muster enough energy to say, "I guess so," "I wish so" or "I hope so." True Christian faith "knows so," beyond any doubt, guess or wistful wish. There is a wrong mindset today that we can't be certain and sure about the will and purposes of God. Beloved, this is the only thing we are to be sure about - - God floods us with supernatural wisdom every time we ask in certainty (Jas. 1:5-8). It is time for instability, uncertainty and shoulder-shrugging to be cast into the sea. Being unsure and indecisive is not a sign of spirituality. It is a sign of double-minded unbelief.

Do you want to know where bad moods come from? They come from uncertainty, doubt, dread and wavering. Christianity is the cure to every doubt, clarity for every confusion and order for every chaos. God wants you to be sure about Jesus, sure about God's good nature, sure about your future, sure about your conversations, sure about your work, sure about your ministry and sure about your relationships. Here, I am not talking about cocky or arrogant man-made confidence which always crashes and burns. Rather, I am talking about the gift of God which allows us the greatest ability of all - - to confidently hear and confidently respond to our indwelling Christ.

Conventional wisdom says that bad moods are to be expected. They cycle in and out. Get used to it. Don't trust your feelings. Just learn to weather them. I have heard it preached a thousand times that we are not to trust our feelings, that faith is walking in what we know and not in what we feel. Sounds good, but is it true? Is it God's best for us to be continually victimized by our emotions? Are our emotions doomed to Jekyll and Hyde mood swings, fickle like the weather and unreliable as a warped bow? No!

So many teach and preach today that we are not to trust our emotions. I think there is a higher level of faith. The goal is to trust God <u>for</u> our emotions - - all of them. Certainly we are not to be led by our emotions when they contradict the Word of the Lord. Rebellious emotions, like rebellious thoughts, should be taken captive to the obedience of Christ. Our emotions make up a big part of our mood. They are vitally important. Emotional consistency and constancy are key parts of *The Jesus Mood*. This is what allows us to be confident. "Confidence" is both a mental and emotional state, or better put - - a mood. If we don't "think" confidently, then we really aren't confident. If we don't "feel" confident, then we really aren't confident. While we are not to be led solely <u>by</u> emotions, we can be led continually <u>for</u> our emotions. We can find mental and emotional certainty. This is the mind of Christ we have been given along with the love of God shed abroad in our hearts by the Holy Ghost (1 Cor. 2:16; Rom. 5:5).

Are you ready to be sure? Eternally sure? Absolutely sure? Unhesitatingly sure? Unflinchingly sure? And, most importantly, justifiably and accurately sure?

If you are ready for a voyage to certainty, then *The Jesus Mood* is for you. My quest for certainty began almost twenty years ago when I became a Christian. In the last ten years, I have discovered a treasure of "certainty" beyond compare. This treasure is not financial - - though it brings timely harvests of material needs. This treasure is not social - - though it brings greater intimacy to all relationships. This treasure is not physical - - though it strengthens mental, emotional and bodily health.

Simply put, this treasure is spiritual - - an inner certainty resulting in an outer manifestation of the Kingdom of God. This book maps this treasure. As with all true treasure, it can be found only in the limitless life and perfect character of Jesus Christ. Jesus is the only ultimate mood-enhancer!

Jesus had something. This something made him different from all other religious leaders, all other Jews and all other human beings. Obviously, Jesus was divinely different in that He was both fully God and fully man at the same time. Yet, even within His full manhood, He constantly had something nobody else could maintain - - certainty. He was supremely confident in who He was, what He could do, what He would do and how He would do it. The people were astonished at His mood of certainty (Matt. 7:28-29).

But, Jesus' certainty all rested on one point and one point only. Jesus was sure He could and would hear the voice of His Heavenly Father at all times and in all places (Jn. 5:19, 30). Jesus did not follow the voice of His own will. Jesus followed the voice of His Abba-Father which lived in His heart. As His Father lovingly commanded Jesus through continual heart promptings, Jesus obeyed in flawless and resolute tones of authoritative confidence. Jesus' confidence was not in Himself, but rather in the voice of God which indwelt Him.

Before Jesus could speak with confidence to perform miracles, He first had to confidently listen to His Father's voice. He had to think in confident terms about His Father's nature and character. He had to be confident that what He heard His Father say to do was guaranteed to work successfully. Then and only then could Jesus confidently speak and do His Father's will.

Since I have studied Jesus' relentless confidence level and His own ability to always hear God the Father's voice, I have discovered the best news of all - - Jesus has made it possible for us to have His same confidence level to hear the Holy Spirit's voice in our own hearts. Beloved, can you grasp the enormity of this truth? *The Jesus Mood* already lives in us as born-again believers. We can be sure. Perfectly sure. Totally sure. Boldly sure. Of what? Of hearing the certain voice of the certain God through the certain faith of the certain Son. Hallelujah! Let this quest for certainty begin now.

Chapter 1
What is the Jesus Mood?

A boy awakes in the middle of the night. He sees a shadow lurking at the window. A dark stranger has entered his room. The boy screams for his father down the hall.

Now stop! Let's examine the boy's mindset. Does the boy cry, "Dad, will you please help me?"; or does he exclaim, "Dad, I wish you would help me!"; or does he scream to himself, "Dad might help me if he is in a good mood!" Do any of these statements accurately reflect the boy's true attitude toward his father?

No! No true son would speak in any of these above-described ways about a loving father. The son would never have to cajole, beg, wish or wonder about his father's willingness to help him. The son knows his father's nature is always ready, willing and able to help in time of peril. The son would shout in authoritative tones, **"Dad, help me!"** This tone of command is not based on the boy's confidence in himself, but rather in the boy's confidence in his dad's character. The son knows the father's love will always come - - no exceptions. In fact, it is unthinkable to the boy that his father would ever fail to come speedily.

The boy is indeed commanding his father to help him. However, the boy is not commanding from a sense of superiority <u>over</u> his father, but rather is commanding from a sense of security <u>with</u> his father. The boy's security is not based on a "spoiled brat" mentality that, "Daddy will give me anything and everything I want." The boy's security is based on what his father has <u>already</u> provided him - - love, nurturing, tenderness, sacrifice, friendship, protection, joy and wisdom. The son simply knows the father too well to doubt his will to be an ever present help in time of need. The son knows that there is no reluctance in his father's heart to save him from any dark intruders' evil designs.

If earthly sons can have this mindset toward their fathers, how much more, more, more should we spiritual sons be able to foster and develop this attitude toward our Heavenly Father. There are always dark intruders stalking our souls seeking to rob, kill and destroy every good thing in our lives. Sometimes the dark intruder is our own rebellious flesh man seeking to revive lust and pride in our lives. Sometimes the dark intruder is a demonic foe seeking to defile us with sin, sickness or accusation. Still other times, the dark intruders can be other men operating in fleshly or Satanic power.

The point is that we are always in peril. Therefore, we should always have this same mindset that the boy used in calling on his father to save him. We should be able to say in complete confidence, "Abba-Father, help me!" We have, after all, received a spirit which cries, "Abba-Father" (Gal. 4:6). Abba is an Aramaic term of endearment, akin to "daddy," by which a faithful son refers to a beloved father. This heart-cry is based on knowing the character and nature of God the Father as always and only good. Our Abba is our hero who lovingly hefts us up on His mighty shoulders and proudly carries us through all trials and tribulations we face. Jesus always had this same view of the Heavenly Father. He lived on Abba's shoulders at all times and in all places. He commanded the power of His Father because His Father's love always already commanded Him. Let me say this clearly and precisely. Jesus' intimate and working knowledge of His Father's absolute goodness enabled Him to <u>brim</u> with confidence in, toward and through any situation.

Of course, throughout the ages, men and women of God have also temporarily displayed great surges of confidence toward God to save them from dark intruders. David vs. Goliath. Moses vs. Pharaoh. Elijah vs. the Prophets of Baal. Samson vs. the Philistines. These Old Testament saints all had instances of perfect confidence toward God to allow them great victories over strong enemies. These episodes were brief but spectacular. When these sudden "confidence moods" seized these souls by the Spirit of the Lord, they were empowered and enabled to perform acts of supernatural heroism. There are certainly times in our lives as Christians when we have felt supernaturally strengthened to perform acts of heroism in times of need. The tragedy comes when we crash back to fleshly failure soon thereafter. These periods of spiritual victory always fall prey to eventual moods of apathy, lust or pride. David and Samson fell to lust. Moses fell to anger. Elijah fell to depression. We too fall far too often to giants of lust, Philistines of pride, Pharaohs of anger and fleshly prophets of discouragement.

Why? Why can't we seem to abide in continual intimacy and victory with God? Is life meant to be a roller coaster of frequent failure and occasional victory? Or, have we missed something? As with all things, Jesus is the answer. Jesus is our model. Jesus is our key - - a living key Who now indwells the heart of every member of the body of Christ. That key is *The Jesus Mood*.

Jesus was always empowered and enabled to speak and act righteously. He cast out devils, calmed storms, walked through closed doors, escaped mobs and performed miracles at the drop of the hat. His walk was a mountain climb, not a roller coaster. Always up, up and away to greater things. Jesus' mood of ever-increasing hope, confidence and boldness reveals the very mood of God.

David failed to abide continually in the mood of God. Moses failed. Elijah failed. Samson failed. We too fail when we try to abide in God within our own righteousness - - our own will, our own strength and our own character. Yet, Jesus lived continually <u>in</u> and <u>with</u> the mood of His Heavenly Father.

The Father sent His Son into the world to impart the true mood of God into men. No longer would men have to struggle with endless cycles of doubt and despair. The Old Testament roller coaster spirituality was passed. The New and better Covenant brings a new and better mood.

The Jesus Mood is a double entendre. It obviously speaks in the first instance to "mood" as Jesus' unique blend of attitudes, emotions and passions. In this sense, mood is the overall "mode of being" at any particular time. Mood in this sense can be good or bad, courageous or fearful, apathetic or passionate, light-hearted or heavy-hearted. Jesus' mood in this sense was always righteousness, peace and joy in the Holy Spirit.

However, mood also has a related meaning in grammatical usage. Here, mood refers to the attitude of the speaker toward the verb or action being expressed. Mood speaks to the perception of the speaker toward reality. Mood is a mindset which reveals the speaker's faith toward the verb being used. Some moods speak to what currently appears to be happening. Other moods speak to what might occur. Still others speak to what they merely wish would occur. However, there is one special mood which authoritatively commands that the verb's action must occur - - this is *The Jesus Mood* of imperative faith - - this is the mood of a Son who can confidently call out anytime and any place, "Dad, help me!"

The Four Mood Brothers

The New Testament has four basic moods in the original Greek text - - indicative, subjunctive, optative and imperative. Fancy sounding words but profoundly simple meanings. I intend to show that true New Testament faith resides only and always in the imperative mood. *The Jesus Mood* is the imperative mood and only the imperative mood. In contrast, fallen man lives continually stranded in the first three moods listed above. These three mental moods make up the Knowledge of the Tree of Good and Evil and cause us to suffer sin, sickness, oppression, depression and destruction. These three moods (indicative, subjunctive, optative) collectively comprise the deadly dynamic of "Duality" - - a concept a later chapter will be devoted to unraveling. The goal of this book is to help deliver you from the three moods of Duality into the imperative mood of Jesus.

Let's first define terms. The indicative mood is the speaker's opinion of simple fact - - in other words, what "appears" to be the state of "current reality." For example, "John is sick," "John needs to be healed," or "John is not getting better." All are examples of the indicative mood. (Note: The indicative mood can be blessed for Christians who walk not by sight but by faith. Faith's indicative can be righteous <u>if</u> it is based on Heavenly reality. "God reigns" or "God is great" are blessed indicatives based not on visible appearances but on spiritual reality grasped by the heart. The problem is that most men are guided by the earthly indicative rather than the Heavenly indicative.)

The subjunctive mood is the speaker's mindset that the verb's action "might" happen. It is the mood of conditionality - - the mood of "if." For example, "God <u>might</u> heal John <u>if</u> it's His will," or "God <u>might</u> heal John <u>if</u> John repents of his sins," or "God <u>might</u> heal John <u>if</u> we only pray long and hard enough."

The optative mood is the speaker's mindset of what he "wishes" would happen. It is nothing more than a wished for possibility. For example, "I wish God would heal John," or "I wish John would get better," or "I wish God would show us how to heal John."

The imperative mood is the mood of command and demand. It is the unlocking and unleashing of potential power into current and active "now" power. It is the will of the speaker imposing itself upon a situation. For example, "John, be healed!" or "John, take up your mat and walk!" or "John, be made whole!" This is the here and now mood. It is the mood of authority and certainty. It is *The Jesus Mood*. The following poem helps to highlight the essence of these moods.

The Jesus Mood

There were four Greek brothers with the last name Mood,
Who had different thoughts toward the verbs they used.

Three were like their mother and were quite unsure,
Whether the verbs they said must or must not occur.

Only one was like their father and knew beyond all doubt,
That the verb off the tongue had all of daddy's clout.

All four Mood brothers were put to the test,
And faced the challenge of who knew verbs best.

The challenge was set in a land lost in pitch black,
Which Mood would speak best the light to bring back.

The first three brothers all like dear mother,
Accepted the challenge one after another.

Brother Subjunctive Mood stepped up to the plate,
And said, "Light might come, maybe soon or maybe late."

Brother Optative Mood was the next son to spout,
"I wish, wish, wish, wish some light would come out."

Brother Indicative Mood, the last like his mom,
Said, "It is dark, I wonder if light ever will come."

None of these three Moods changed the color of black,
Though their words were all nice, the light still did lack.

The father of Moods smiled at his fourth son,
Who always winked back at his dad in good fun.

Brother Imperative Mood jumped up to the mike,
And declared very simply, "Let there be light!"

Light did not wait, it launched its attack,
Darkness did flee back to the land of pure lack.

Brother Imperative Mood left his brothers in the dust,
Because their uncertain hearts did rob them of trust.

So when your heart picks a mood with which it will link,
Look first for daddy's smile and don't forget to wink.

Jesus' Amazing Use of the Imperative Mood

I was shocked several years ago when I discovered that Jesus originally spoke the Lord's prayer in Matthew 6:5-13 in the aorist tense and the imperative mood. The Greek aorist tense carries with it the idea of complete and instantaneous action applied to a specific matter. Coupled with the Greek imperative mood, this statement orders immediate and complete action toward a specific situation. Jesus teaches us to literally pray this "way" in the original Greek:

Thy name be hallowed now!

Thy Kingdom come now!

Thy will be done on Earth as it is in Heaven now!

Give us this moment our daily bread!

Forgive us now once and for all!

Deliver us from evil now!

Jesus also prayed in the imperative in John 17 when Jesus commanded His Father in the following statements:

Glorify Your Son!

Father, glorify me in Your presence!

Holy Father, protect them by the power of Your name!

Sanctify them by the truth!

Also, at Jesus' most painful moments on the Cross, He still used the imperative mood to order mercy on all men:

Father, forgive them; for they know not what they do! Lk. 23:34.

All of the above statements Jesus spoke in the imperative mood. They are all commands - - but to whom? To the Father? Yes, but remember, only in the same way the boy cried in the imperative, "Dad, help me!" Jesus only commanded these statements to the Father because He was secure and sure that this was already the Father's heart toward all of us. To pray in the imperative is merely to recognize the immediate urgency of our non-stop need to call, "Abba-Father, help me!" Only with this intimate understanding of God's nature can the magnificence of the following verse be properly grasped: **"Thus saith the LORD, the Holy One of Israel, and his Maker, Ask me of things to come concerning my sons, and concerning the work of my hands command ye me."** Is. 45:11. Do you see? Sons who intimately and steadfastly know their Father God's goodness <u>can</u> command Him concerning <u>all</u> creation. We are only commanding <u>out</u> of us what our knowledge of God's heroic love has already commanded <u>in</u> us.

But, more than just speaking to the Father, the imperative mood also "commands" our own thoughts, emotions and beliefs to conform to the will of God. As an example, when David prayed Psalm 103:1-5, he was <u>commanding</u> his own soul to conform to the dominion and goodness of God. **"Bless the LORD, O my soul: and all that is within me, bless his holy name. Bless the LORD, O my soul, and forget not all his benefits: Who forgiveth all thine iniquities; who healeth all thy diseases; Who redeemeth thy life from destruction; who crowneth thee with lovingkindness and tender mercies; Who satisfieth thy mouth with good things; so that thy youth is renewed like the eagle's."** Ps. 103:1-5.

Do you see? In the first instance, the imperative mood musters our soul to unify its focus on God. Next, the imperative mood commands the goodness of our Father to manifest in our situation. Finally, the imperative mood commands our circumstances to actually bow and be reconciled to the will of God. <u>Our</u> use of the imperative mood is actually just our wholehearted "bearing witness" of God's imperative salvation already given to the world through the life of Jesus Christ. It is <u>our</u> "amen" to <u>God's</u> "yes!"

The imperative mood is wholeheartedness. The imperative mood is asking <u>without</u> doubting. The imperative mood is <u>only</u> believing. The imperative mood is the faith <u>of</u> Jesus. The imperative mood is God's landing pad into this realm. Anything less than the imperative mood is lukewarm, double-minded and unbelief. These lesser moods (subjunctive, optative, indicative) hinder and obstruct God's presence from fully manifesting into this realm. It is our way of not believing and trusting in God's love, goodness and power.

The Lord's Prayer is so important because Jesus clearly instructs us "how" to pray - - to pray in the "way" of the imperative mood. Jesus modeled not only imperative praying but also imperative ministry. He didn't demonstrate an "underwhelming" God who might be convinced or cajoled to show mercy and salvation. No, Jesus flooded Israel with an "overwhelming" God always ready, instantly willing and infinitely able to heal, save, forgive, bless, prosper and empower all who believe. Jesus imperatively ministered the imperative will of His imperative Father through the imperative power of the Holy Ghost. Consider the following imperative mood statements by Jesus at various times during His ministry:

Go in peace, and be whole of thy plague! Mk. 5:34.

According to your faith be it unto you! Matt. 9:29.

Be not afraid, only believe! Mk. 5:36.

Rise, take up thy bed, and walk! Jn. 5:8.

Be not faithless, but believing! Jn. 20:27.

I am willing, be clean! Matt. 8:3.

Jesus imperatively commanded demons to depart (Lk. 4:36), angels to arrive (Matt. 26:53), fevers to go (Lk. 4:39), wholeness to come (Mk. 5:34), deadly storms to stop (Matt. 8:26), dead hearts to start (Jn. 11:43), violent men to fall down (Jn. 18:6), sick men to get up (Jn. 5:8) and Satan himself to back up (Mk. 8:33).

Notice in all of this what Jesus never did. He never "wished" a miracle or "begged" a deliverance. He never said "no" to a need, "never" to a request, "maybe" to a prayer or "someday" to a desperate plea (Acts 10:38). The point is that all ministry Jesus performed was done in the imperative - - the "now" mood - - the "here" mood - - the "must" mood - - the "power" mood.

In fact, Jesus not only told us to pray always in the imperative mood, Jesus not only prayed in the imperative mood Himself, Jesus not only commanded away *demons\sickness\ nature* in the imperative, but Jesus also esteemed and commended the imperative mood in those who came to Him for help.

Jesus gave special commendation to the imperative mindset displayed by the woman with the blood issue who pushed through a throng of people <u>knowing</u> that she would be healed as she touched Jesus' garment (Lk. 8:43-48). She didn't even have to wait for an official response from Jesus - - it was automatic. Jesus gave parables highlighting the importance of imperative qualities of importunity (Lk. 11:5-13) and demanding prayer (Lk. 18:1-8). Jesus also greatly commended the Syrophenician woman's spirit who would not take no for an answer concerning the Lord's willingness to heal her daughter (Mk. 7:24-30). Jesus was blessed and impressed by those people who would not take no for an answer, or perhaps better put, people who would only take yes for an answer!

Consider the following imperative statements in the original Greek made by those who commanded Jesus' help <u>because</u> they were confident in His heroic nature:

> *Speak the Word only, and my servant shall be healed!* Matt. 8:8.

> *Lord, I believe; help thou mine unbelief!* Mk. 9:24.

> *Lord, help me!* Matt. 15:25.

> *Have mercy on us, O Lord, thou Son of David!* Matt. 20:30.

> *In the name of Jesus Christ of Nazareth rise up and walk!* Acts 3:6.

The first example above involves the Roman Centurion's faith. This passage highlights the pleasure the Lord takes in those who understand imperative faith. This Centurion understood imperative faith, *The Jesus Mood*, better than anyone in Israel - - and Jesus was amazed. **"And when Jesus was entered into Capernaum, there came unto him a centurion, beseeching him, and saying, Lord, my servant lieth at home sick of the palsy, grievously tormented. And**

Jesus saith unto him, I will come and heal him. The centurion answered and said, Lord, I am not worthy that thou shouldest come under my roof: but speak the word only, and my servant shall be healed. For I am a man under authority, having soldiers under me: and I say to this man, Go, and he goeth; and to another, Come, and he cometh; and to my servant, Do this, and he doeth it. When Jesus heard it, he marvelled, and said to them that followed, Verily I say unto you, I have not found so great faith, no, not in Israel. And I say unto you, That many shall come from the east and west, and shall sit down with Abraham, and Isaac, and Jacob, in the kingdom of heaven. But the children of the kingdom shall be cast out into outer darkness: there shall be weeping and gnashing of teeth. And Jesus said unto the centurion, Go thy way; and as thou hast believed, so be it done unto thee. And his servant was healed in the selfsame hour." Matt. 8:5-13.

The Roman Centurion did not need Jesus to prove anything by actually coming to his house to heal his servant. He knew Jesus' imperative could command <u>any</u> healing from <u>any</u> place to <u>any</u> person at <u>any</u> time. Do you see? Our imperative mood toward God anticipates, accepts and eagerly commands God's imperative mood toward us. We can only be imperative toward God because He is first imperative toward us.

It is crucial to understand that in Greek grammar "questions" are usually asked in the subjunctive mood (Mk. 6:25,37; 16:3; Rom. 10:14; 1 Cor. 11:22), the indicative mood (Jn. 1:19,38; Matt. 16:13; Mk. 1:24), or the optative mood (Lk. 1:29; Acts 8:31; Lk. 3:15; 6:11; 22:23; Acts 5:24; 17:11). Questions under these three moods are asked when the answer or response sought is truly unknown or uncertain to the asker. By contrast, questions asked in the imperative mood are normally asked only where the answer or response sought is <u>already</u> known and certain to the asker.

The imperative mood is an unusual form of a question when addressing a superior, which explains why the Greeks never so used it. Rightly used, it would be the equivalent of a boss asking a subordinate in a polite but insistent tone to bring him a cup of coffee. Though a request in form, it is clearly a command to perform a duty. Conversely, it would normally be poor form for an employee to use the imperative to ask the boss to bring him some coffee - - unless of course the employee was also a loving son or spouse of the boss who knew the boss was on the way to the coffee machine anyway and wouldn't mind a bit. A subordinate would not use the imperative mood with a superior unless a very special relationship existed.

This explains why no other Greek literature ever uses the imperative mood to describe men addressing or praying to their false gods, but the New Testament is full of occasions where believers use the imperative mood when addressing or praying to the true God (Matt. 6:9-13; Matt. 15:25; Mk. 9:24; Lk. 11:2-4; 22:42). A pagan Greek could not address Apollo or Zeus in the imperative because he had no idea how his fickle god would respond, but, hallelujah, as Christians we have an intimate relationship with Jesus which enables us to know our God <u>always</u> responds to our imperative faith. How amazing it is that Jesus imperatively commanded us to imperatively pray to the Heavenly Father in Jesus' own imperative name guaranteed to bring imperative results!

There are five words in the Greek New Testament which we usually translate in the English Bible as "ask." Punthanomai means "to ask without knowing the answer." Erotao means "a request for favor." Zeteo means "a search for something hidden." Deomai means "to beg an urgent need." We are not to use any of these forms of asking in Jesus' name. The word for "ask" in the following verses is "aiteo" and means "strictly a demand of something due" (see *Strong's* 4441 and 523).

> "Verily, verily, I say unto you, He that believeth on me, the works that I do shall he do also; and greater works than these shall he do; because I go unto my Father. And whatsoever ye shall ask in my name, that will I do, that the Father may be glorified in the Son. If ye shall ask any thing in my name, I will do it." Jn. 14:12-14.

> "If ye abide in me, and my words abide in you, ye shall ask what ye will, and it shall be done unto you." Jn. 15:7.

> "Ye have not chosen me, but I have chosen you, and ordained you, that ye should go and bring forth fruit, and that your fruit should remain: that whatsoever ye shall ask of the Father in my name, he may give it you." Jn. 15:16.

> "And in that day ye shall ask me nothing. Verily, verily, I say unto you, Whatsoever ye shall ask the Father in my name, he will give it you. Hitherto have ye asked nothing

in my name: <u>ask</u>, and ye shall receive, that
your joy may be full." Jn. 16:23-24.

Do you see? Praying in the imperative is the same thing as
asking in Jesus' name. We are not begging, wishing, seeking
or inquiring with our verbal prayers. We are commanding
<u>our</u> immediate sphere of influence to come under the domin-
ion of God's goodness.

Let's Play *Jeopardy!*

This dynamic is similar to the well-known television game
Jeopardy. Here, the scholarly and wise host reads the "answers" to an unknown "question" to three contestants. The
first contestant to "buzz in" and imperatively declare the correct question wins the money. Do you see? The contestants
are stating questions for which they <u>already</u> know the answer. They are not asking questions they don't know, but
rather are ordering the appropriate question to line up with
the already given answer. The proper imperative question releases the blessing when lined up with the proper imperative
answer. While the blessing in the television game is money,
the blessings for spiritual *Jeopardy* involve all things for life
and godliness.

As stated earlier, Jesus instructed the disciples to pray in the
imperative mood in Matthew 6:5-13. In verse 8, right in the
middle of this passage, Jesus tells us that the Father always
already knows our needs before we ask. In His pre-knowl-
edge, God also has always already pre-responded with an
imperative "Yes!" (2 Cor. 1:19-20). Just as in *Jeopardy*, in
the Kingdom of God the answer precedes the question. We
just imperatively buzz in with the blessed question which
links to and releases the manifestation of the Lord's pre-pro-

vided answer. **"And it shall come to pass, that before they call, I will answer; and while they are yet speaking, I will hear."** Is. 65:24.

Let's play spiritual *Jeopardy*! The Holy Spirit is our intelligent and wise counselor who continually speaks answers to us. "Now we have received, not the spirit of the world, but the Spirit which is of God; that we might know the things freely given to us of God." 1 Cor. 2:12. These answers may be prompted by Scripture, prophecy, Rhema or prayer. These answers are the exceeding great and precious promises of God which provide us all things for life and godliness (2 Pet. 1:3-4). However, God's promises are not about what He will do, but about what God has already done in and through Christ. How much more exciting is the promise that you have already inherited a fortune than is a promise that you will inherit one day in the future?

If I promised to pay you a million dollars sometime in the future, you would be understandably skeptical. But, if I informed you I had already deposited a million dollars in your name, you would quickly seek verification and access to those funds. How much more should we immediately seek access to the Gospel promises of our already deposited "riches of the glory of His inheritance in the saints" in Christ Jesus (Eph. 1:18).

Beloved, God has, according to Hebrews 4, rested from all His works because He has already pre-responded in His foreknowledge to our every need (Rom. 8:28-30; 1 Cor. 10:13). If I were all-powerful and I had foreknowledge of what my children truly needed and wanted in their heart of hearts, then I would pre-provide everything they needed for life and godliness. My provision would be waiting for them ahead of time at arm's length as they were able to realize, recognize and receive it.

However, my blessings would not be served on a platter of privilege which required <u>nothing</u> from my children. Rather, my provision would be served on a platter of ever-increasing purity which could only be partaken of by a good and honest heart. I wouldn't jam it down their throats whether they wanted it or not. But I would have all my blessings primed and available for their use when they were in the right and ready mood. If I as an earthly father would do this, how much more does the Heavenly Father operate in this dynamic? The Word of God's provision is always already <u>near</u> us, in our hearts and in our mouths, waiting for us to realize, recognize and release God's pre-provision for our every need (Rom. 10:8).

Amazingly, Scriptures tell us we have an anointing (unction) from God and we "know all things" (1 Jn. 2:20). Now. This very moment. In other words, God, through His indwelling Spirit, has imbedded within us His own foreknowledge and pre-destiny for our lives. God knows the beginning from the end, and so do we. **"Remember the former things of old: for I am God, and there is none else; I am God, and there is none like me. Declaring the end from the beginning, and from ancient times the things that are not yet done, saying, My counsel shall stand, and I will do all my pleasure."** Is. 46:9-10. We just don't know that we know all things. We have forgotten. This is why true spiritual knowledge is more a matter of remembering what we already know deep down in our spirits than it is of discovering new information by our own mental efforts.

In our fallen state, we have forgotten who we are - - the children of the most high God. We have forgotten our Creator, Heaven's will and Earth's need. This is why we have lost the imperative mood of Jesus. We have forgotten that we are called to reign as kings and priests upon the Earth in full dominion as sons of God (Rev. 5:10).

The Holy Spirit's ministry is to supernaturally restore our memory and refresh our recollection of God's eternal truths. *Spiritual Jeopardy* allows us to first recognize and remember the answer already imbedded in our spirits. From this ready recognition of the perfect answer, we are now primed to imperatively declare the blessed question, the question which catalyzes the answer to fully manifest in this earthly realm. This is how God's pre-destiny becomes our manifest destiny - - by remembering God's foreknowledge of our needs, His pre-response and pre-provision of all our deliverances and our pre-destiny to prevail over every trial of life.

God's answers always precede our questions. GOD'S ANSWER ALWAYS PRECEDES OUR QUESTION! Once we realize this, then our questions are no longer uncertain requests but certain commands which we buzz in and "amen" back in the same imperative tone in which the answers were first given.

As an example, the Holy Spirit may quicken a Scripture to me that I am more than a conqueror through Christ (Rom. 8:37). However, to activate this truth I must buzz in with my imperative question, "What am I now in Christ, this very moment?" Though the form of my statement is a question, the "mood" of my statement is purely imperative. When my imperative question links with the Holy Spirit's imperative answer, then the power of God's victory is released <u>immediately</u> and <u>spontaneously</u> into my NOW!

> "And he said unto them, Which of you shall have a friend, and shall go unto him at midnight, and say unto him, Friend, lend me three loaves; For a friend of mine in his journey is come to me, and I have nothing to set before him? And he from within shall answer and say, Trouble me not: the door is now shut, and my children are with me in bed; I cannot rise and give thee. I say unto you, Though he will not rise and give him, because he is his friend, yet because of his importunity he will rise and give him as many as he needeth. And I say unto you, Ask, and it shall be given you; seek, and ye shall find; knock, and it shall be opened unto you. For every one that asketh receiveth; and he that seeketh findeth; and to him that knocketh it shall be opened. If a son shall ask bread of any of you that is a father, will he give him a stone? or if he ask a fish, will he for a fish give him a serpent? Or if he shall ask an egg, will he offer him a scorpion? If ye then, being evil, know how to give good gifts unto your children: how much more shall your heavenly Father give the Holy Spirit to them that ask him?"
> Lu. 11:5-13.

Jesus tells us in the above passage that we are to "ask, seek, and knock" with "importunity" when we are in need of God's help. "Importunity" is another word for "shame-free bold-ness." Sounds like the imperative mood to me. Don't miss the key to this parable. The man did not open the door to his desperate friend because of their relationship. Rather, the man opened the door of provision because of the knocker's importunity. Likewise, our importunity (shame-free bold-ness) opens Heaven's provision to manifest in this visible realm. God speaks in the imperative mood <u>toward</u> all His children. As soon as we learn to first <u>listen</u> in the imperative and then <u>respond</u> in the imperative, then Heaven's power "shall be" fully "received, found and opened." This parable then, tells us <u>how</u> to approach God - - <u>as</u> a loving friend and Father full of provision - - and <u>with</u> our hearts brimming with boldness and confidence that God will <u>never</u> deny us His abundance (Eph. 3:11-12).

Hitch's Doorstep

Let me share a wonderful metaphor that serves as a parable on the imperative mood. In a recent movie, Will Smith plays a character named Hitch who is a professional romance ex-pert. He tutors men how to effectively court women.

As an example, Hitch instructs a new student how to kiss a woman goodnight at her doorstep. The man must first face the woman. He then is to cross the doorstep 90% toward the woman fully prepared to kiss her. Then, he must pause and allow the woman to respond her 10% across the doorstep to meet his embrace. The man must not cross over 90% of the way, or he will be robbing the woman of her full and free response. Nor must he cross less than the 90%, or the woman will be forced to carry more of the responsibility than she is by nature supposed to bear. The beauty of woman is as a tender responder who melts and delights in her man's arms. The handsomeness of man is as a passionate pursuer who crosses all obstacles to await his lover's response.

Beloved, do you see how beautifully this image fits Heaven and Earth. God, through Jesus Christ, has "always already" crossed 90% through all spiritual obstacles and is waiting <u>now</u> for us as His bride to individually and corporately respond our 10% to the full embrace of the Lord. This Earth needs only to respond to God across the doorstep of men's hearts.

When I say 10%, I obviously am not suggesting to give only a portion of our hearts to God. The 10% refers instead to our <u>first</u> and <u>best</u> heart-focus. I call this the heart-tithe. In the Old Testament, the "tithe" represented the first 10% of Israel's <u>material</u> increase. In the New Testament, I believe the tithe is our heart's prioritized focus on God. It is our first and best effort to vigilantly listen and respond to the Spirit of God indwelling us. This is really all we can do for God - - listen with a willing heart. He does everything else. 10% doesn't refer to the volume of effort, but rather to the <u>quality</u> of our initial readiness to respond. Just as blessed brides are called to be beautiful "responders" to their husbands, we as the bride of Christ are called to be beautiful "responders" to our Lord and husband. We are to be responders, not imitators. Satan seeks to imitate. Jesus seeks to interact. Self-righteousness imitates. True righteousness only responds to the voice of the Father (Jn. 5:19, 30). When we continually tithe our heart's first and best focus, our 10% in other words, then this allows the Holy Spirit free reign to "complete the circuit" of faith by working within us as God's 90% "to will and to do of His good pleasure" (Phil. 2:13).

It is interesting that the word "attention" has "ten" as its word root. Ten is the number which symbolizes the tithe, which Biblically means the first "tenth" of our increase. "Attention" is from the Latin word "attendere" which means "give heed to" or "stretch toward." It has the sense of stretching one's focus toward something. Chaucer used it in the sense of "giving heed." To "attend" someone or something is to "be fully present to wait upon or serve." Amazingly, "attention" is a military cautionary word preparative to giving an IMPERA-TIVE command. A soldier must come to attention before he can receive and then issue orders. Slouching and inattentive soldiers can neither effectively receive <u>nor</u> issue orders. We are told all our lives to "pay attention." This is our heart-tithe, to pay our first-best focus to the Lord by stretching out our heart to Him at all times. The heart-tithe of attention establishes *The Jesus Mood* to now imperatively command reality to likewise "attend" to the Lord's will. This is the Roman Centurion's great revelation - - only soldiers under authority (i.e. those who are at attention) can wield authority (i.e. give true imperatives which must be obeyed). Atten-hut!

Jesus modeled this for us. During His entire life, He remained lip-locked to the Godhead. Jesus fully responded at all times to the Father's initiative toward Him. Jesus imperatively postured His 10% toward the "always already" 90% imperative embrace of His Father. Out of this full embrace, the works and will of God imperatively manifested. Not only did Jesus model the 10% for us, at Pentecost He sent His own 10% to live in us as the unction of the Holy Spirit. Jesus imparts to us His <u>own</u> faith to allow us to <u>fully</u> respond to the Godhead at all times. Jesus doesn't want us to <u>imitate</u> His faith. Jesus wants us to <u>utilize</u> His faith. His faith lives in us by the power of the Holy Spirit and enables us to be fully responsive to God's loving will. So Jesus is not just God's perfect provision from Heaven, He is also Earth's perfect response to God.

Is this possible? Has God "always already" fully extended Himself to us in each and every situation of our lives? Is the only thing lacking our wholehearted (imperative) response to Him across our earthly doorstep? If true, then God has truly rested from His works and is now eagerly waiting for His bride to wake up and respond to His "always already" completed embrace.

Again, it is not just that Jesus modeled the proper way to respond to God's 90% move across our doorstep. Jesus <u>was</u> also the 90% imperative itself sent to Earth from Heaven as the rescuing love of God. Jesus was the Logos, Who in the beginning was <u>with</u> God, <u>was</u> God and Who <u>became</u> flesh and dwelt among us full of grace and truth (Jn. 1:1-14). In other words, Jesus was the Godhead's full and final 90% imperative initiative across fallen creation's doorstep. Jesus' incarnation explained and expressed God's true nature to fallen man as heroic (Jn. 1:18). God came to save every man from every evil! Peace on Earth, good will toward man! This is the acceptable year of the Lord!

Once here on the Earth in His flesh, Jesus then turned around as a man and responded back the perfect 10% across the doorstep to remain in full embrace and submission to the Father at all times. Do you see? Jesus stretched down His sacrifice from Heaven <u>to</u> Earth as the Son of God, then stretched back to Heaven <u>from</u> Earth as the Son of Man, so that we could follow in His wake as sons of men <u>now</u> adopted as sons of God.

Jesus, <u>as the Son of God</u>, was the Heavenly Father's absolute cure for all evil - - sin, sickness and Satanic power (Jn. 3:16-18). But the good news doesn't end here. Jesus, <u>as the Son of Man</u>, actually drank every drop of the cure on our behalf (Jn. 3:13-15; 5:27). Beloved, do you see? Jesus not only came as God from Heaven to rescue you from all evil, but He also as a man accepted the rescue for you on your behalf. His faith of pure reliance and trust now lives in you by the power of the Holy Ghost. You <u>can</u> cross the doorstep. In fact, Jesus has already crossed the doorstep for you. You can embrace God's "always already" presence at all times and in all places just by yielding to Jesus' past completed work as both the Son of God <u>and</u> the Son of Man.

As you yield to God's "always already," you will begin to <u>imperatively</u> recognize, realize and release Jesus' Divine Nature within you. Theologians call this the "propassion" of Christ - - the actual mental and emotional states of Jesus available for our consumption as promised in 2 Peter 1:3-4. This is the fruit of the Spirit - - Jesus' love, Jesus' joy, Jesus' peace, Jesus' longsuffering, Jesus' gentleness, Jesus' goodness, Jesus' faith, Jesus' meekness and Jesus' temperance. This is literally putting on the Lord Jesus (Rom. 13:14). This is living not by <u>your</u> faith but rather the faith <u>of</u> the Son of God (Gal. 2:20). This is staying lip-locked (righteous speech) and heart-locked (righteous love) to the Trinity at all times and in all places. This is *The Jesus Mood*.

Remember! Beware the three non-imperative moods - - optative, indicative and subjunctive. Many have shipwrecked their faith on these rocky crags. Some Christians are stranded in the optative mood of endlessly "wishing" God would do something - - anything - - sometime, somehow, some way. Praying in this mood is essentially just "wishing upon a star." God here is seen as little more than a "wishing well" in Whom we invest our "pocket change" efforts, in return for which we get to "make a wish" which He hopefully will grant. So many Christians have, without consciously realizing it, substituted "wishing" for "believing," "hoping so" for "knowing so," and "shoulder shrugging doubt" for "mountain moving faith." These Christians don't believe <u>on</u> God but merely wish <u>at</u> Him.

Other Christians remain trapped in the indicative mood by continually "walking by sight." They believe only what they see. All reality is processed here with natural thinking and carnal understanding. The indicative mood acknowledges only what is apparent to sense knowledge (i.e. knowledge obtained through our sensory impressions of the external world). This mindset disastrously believes that whatever "is" must be the Lord's will simply because it is. Whatever "appears" carries God's necessary and affirmative stamp of approval, so this mindset says. Thus, death, destruction and disaster all become God's presumed will which we are to automatically resign ourselves to. Rather than speaking <u>to</u> these mountains of oppression and casting them into the sea, we instead stand paralyzed and passively allow the mountains to fall on us. This tragic mood never hopes, believes and insists on something better. Rather, it is enslaved to earthly "realism," which is dominated by routine, regularity and rules. Life here becomes rote and repetitive. What appears today will appear again tomorrow, and the next day, and the next. The book of Ecclesiastes reveals this repeating pattern of "vanity" which infects the fallen thinking and fallen lives of men. There is in this mindset an endless cycle of true despair, false hope and ultimate emptiness. "The thing that hath been, it is that which shall be; and that which is done is that which shall be done:

and there is no new thing under the sun. . . .Vanity of vanities, saith the Preacher, vanity of vanities; all is vanity." Eccl. 1:2, 9. While this vanity may be the reality of those who live "under the sun," praise God it is not the reality of those who live "under the Son," the Son of God Whom we serve in newness of life and with joy unspeakable and full of glory - - in other words, those who abide in *The Jesus Mood.*

Lastly, many believers are snared in the subjunctive mood of "if." God will bless us, this mindset says, if we only obey the law intensely enough, travail in prayer long enough, read the Bible completely enough and sing praise songs loud enough. This mood makes God's love and help <u>conditional</u> on our works. We must first obtain God's approval before we can be confident He will help or bless us. Healings, miracles and blessings must be "earned" with this mood rather than "allowed" by resting in the completed works of God. The imperative mood of Jesus is built on the foundation of the completed work of the Cross. *The Jesus Mood* comes from the certainty of <u>not</u> what God <u>will</u> do, but rather comes from the certainty of what God has <u>already</u> done. This crucial topic is discussed in depth in the next chapter.

When the father of the demonized man brought his convulsing son to Jesus in Mark 9, Jesus encouraged the father, "If you can believe, all things are possible to him who believes." Mk. 9:23. The father knew that his own heart still had a level of uncertainty, and that this lack of confidence would hinder the sought-after healing. "Immediately the father of the child cried out and said with tears, 'Lord, I believe; help my unbelief!'" Do you see? This desperate father knew that he himself had to be certain and <u>only</u> certain in Jesus' willingness and power to heal his son. In other words, the man recognized that he was not <u>yet</u> in the imperative mood for the actual healing. However, he was in the imperative mood <u>enough</u> to ask Jesus to help him remove his own uncertainty and unbelief. He asked Jesus, in the imperative mood, to remove all doubt from his own heart. Jesus did. The boy was healed. Beloved, we too must recognize that if <u>any</u> doubt lingers in our hearts, then we are not in the imperative mood and should expect to receive nothing from God. When we recognize our own doubt, we must take a step back and find the imperative mood by asking the Lord to cast out our own unbelief. Every man has been given the measure of faith to always ask <u>this</u> much in the imperative mood - - "I believe Lord, help my unbelief!" You may not always be able to <u>instantly</u> find the imperative mood for healings, miracles and wonders, but, beloved, you always can instantly and imperatively ask the Lord to help you cast out your unbelief - - always. And He will. The Holy Spirit's ministry to our souls is to convince, convince and convince. The Holy Spirit "certifies," which means "to attest as certain," the Word of God, the purposes of God, the power of God, the victory of Jesus and the defeat of Satan (Jn. 16:7-15).

Step One, then, is to always imperatively yield to the Holy Spirit's inner "convincing" which purges out any and all lingering unbelief which may have accumulated or seeks to accumulate in our hearts. Next, Step Two is to imperatively work the works of God from a fully persuaded heart and a faith-releasing tongue. This is the certainty found only and always in *The Jesus Mood.*

Chapter 2
Always Already

T ake your shoes off. Let's revisit the burning bush. Our quest for *The Jesus Mood* begins on this holiest of grounds. Here, Moses was given the eternal name of God - - Yahweh. This name holds and reveals a great mystery about God.

Exodus 3 tells the story. Moses, while tending his sheep at Mount Horeb, beheld a burning bush which was not being consumed by the flames. Out of this bush the voice of God commanded Moses to take off his shoes "for the place whereon thou standest is holy ground" (Ex. 3:5). This tells us the name of God is holy ground and that we must humbly shed our soles and souls of all man-made barriers to truly prepare ourselves to receive His name.

The Lord then reveals His name to Moses as "I AM THAT I AM," literally Yahweh, and that this will be "my name forever, and this is my memorial unto all generations" (Ex. 3:14-15). All generations are to remember, recognize and realize that Yahweh is the name of God. For the Hebrews, the "name" was not an arbitrary title but represented the essential essence, character and authority of a person.

So, what does the name "Yahweh" represent? Translations range from "I AM THAT I AM" to "I AM AND CONTINUE TO BE PRESENT." But, we must remember to add the concept of "forever" to this name as the Lord commanded in verse 15. Thus, Yahweh means "forever already present," or as I like to say "Always Already." God is always already aware, always already prepared, always already empowered, always already merciful, always already willing and always already available to save, heal and deliver us.

German theologians note that the Hebrew word "Yah or Jah" ("I am") is linguistically related to the German word "Ja," which means "yes." From this angle, God essentially says to Moses, "I AM YES," "I AM THE ETERNAL YES," "I AM THE EVER-PRESENT ALWAYS ALREADY YES AND AMEN!"

Isn't this glorious? Does the Bible support the "Eternal Yesness" of God's nature? Oh, yes: **"For the Son of God, Jesus Christ, who was preached among you by us, even by me and Silvanus and Timotheus, was not yea and nay, but in him was yea. For all the promises of God in him are yea, and in him Amen, unto the glory of God by us."** 2 Cor. 1:19-20. Yes, Yes, Yes! Always only in Christ, but in Him always already "Yes!"

Martin Buber, author of the classic *I and Thou*, adds another beautiful insight into interpreting the name "Yahweh." Buber traces the word back to "Yah, Yahu or Yahuvah" and paraphrases it as "He, this one, this is it, oh he!" Thus, the name Yahweh is an exclamation of joyful recognition uttered in a moment of religious ecstasy. "God cannot be properly named, only exclaimed." Buber abbreviates the definition of "Yahweh" to be "the one." Yahweh, then, is an experiential <u>response</u> to God revealing His presence to man. If Buber would allow me the latitude, I think a more contemporary expression of "Yahweh" would be, "Oh, You are the one I've been waiting for - - the one I never knew I always wanted. You are the Yes to my heart's question - - my eternal Yes!"

When Peter pleased Jesus with his confession that Jesus was "the Christ, the Son of the living God," Jesus said this would be the rock upon which the Church would be built (Matt. 16:15-19). The rock here was not the confession itself, but Peter's exclamation of <u>experiencing</u> God's presence <u>in</u> Jesus as revealed <u>by</u> the Father. Without the experience of God's presence, Peter's confession would be meaningless. Our proper use of Jesus' name will always be based on a "who" interaction <u>with</u> Him, not a "what" interaction with some idea or opinion <u>about</u> Him.

So what's the conclusion of the matter? When we approach the Lord's name (His nature and presence) with our shoes removed (all man-made opinions, pride and self-reliance), then we will behold the ETERNAL ALWAYS ALREADY YES OF GOD!

So, what is the problem? What is it that keeps deceiving us into maintaining a non-imperative view of God? Why do we doubt God's willingness and availability to save us from every evil in our lives? Why are we double-minded toward God, thinking one day He might heal us and another day that

He might not? Our walk with God is not a petal-plucking game where we alternatively think or say, "He loves me, He loves me not," "He heals me, He heals me not." This thinking is dangerously double-minded and will always result in spiritual failure.

The Scriptures say that a double-minded man should expect to receive <u>nothing</u> from God. **"But let him ask in faith, nothing wavering. For he that wavereth is like a wave of the sea driven with the wind and tossed. For let not that man think that he shall receive any thing of the Lord. A double minded man is unstable in all his ways."** Jas. 1:6-8. Double-mindedness means non-imperative. It is the mindset of maybe, if and perhaps. It laments what is, wishes for what could be and laboriously plans for what might be. Again, this mindset is lost and trapped in the indicative, optative and subjunctive moods as discussed in Chapter One.

Before we can live in the imperative mood - - *The Jesus Mood* - - we must ensure we have the right image of God. A. W. Tozer famously said that what comes to your mind when you think about God is the most important thing in your life. A non-imperative view of God brings non-imperative results. An imperative view of God releases the windows of Heaven to pour out the blessings and deliverances of Yahweh.

I believe the major cause of our non-imperative double-mindedness is a fundamental flaw in our view of God. This flaw causes us to doubt that God is only and always good. Tozer rightly believed that we tend "by a secret law of the soul" to gravitate toward and grow to resemble our mental image of God. High thoughts of God bring us into pure worship and a sanctified walk, while low thoughts of God defile our hearts and corrupt our walk.

The lowest thought of God is that He creates, causes or allows evil. The highest thought of God is that He opposes evil in any form and that Jesus Christ is the revealed "cure" and "disallowance" of every form of evil. In Christ, God has always already disallowed every evil - - past, present and future. The only reason evil still exists is due to our individual and corporate "neglect" of "so great a salvation" (Heb. 2:3).

The Jesus Mood allows us to stop the neglect by diligently attending to the true nature of God with a single-eye and a willing heart. We must re-orient ourselves to the following central truth of the spiritual universe: **"This then is the message which we have heard of him, and declare unto you, that God is light, and in him is no darkness at all."** 1 Jn. 1:5. Armed with the true *nature\name* of God, we are now able to demolish the most destructive stronghold ever to deceive in the mind of man - - that God creates, causes or allows evil.

Does God Allow Evil?

No! Never! Most people don't even ask the question in a blessed way. They normally ask, "Why does God allow evil?" This form of the question is objectionable because it presumes that God does allow evil. At the memorial services for the 9/11 victims, a well-known pastor lamented that he had never received a satisfactory answer to the question, "Why does God allow evil?" The reason there's no satisfactory answer is that it is not a satisfactory question. An unblessed and improper question will always yield an unblessed and improper answer.

The open-hearted and fair way of asking this question is, "Does God allow evil?" In a court of law, the lawyer is not allowed to ask his witness a leading question which already presumes an answer. A lawyer can't ask his own witness, "Why do you beat your wife?" The reason is that this question already presumes that the witness <u>does</u> beat his wife. Justice and fairness demand that an open inquiry must first establish whether or not a witness does in fact beat his wife. If we can be so fair with human conduct, how much more just and open-hearted should we be with God's nature?

For instance, what if God doesn't allow evil? In fact, what if God only and always disallows evil in all its various forms? In fact, what if God has <u>already</u> disallowed every evil that ever has or ever will occur? Do Scriptures support such a view? Yes! They not only support it, they demand it.

Point One: God Does Not Allow Evil

The term "theodicy" refers to a branch of theology which deals with the justification of God's goodness in the presence of evil. All theodicy must begin and end with James 1:13-17. It is the most specific statement in the New Testament with regard to God's relationship to evil.

> **"Let no man say when he is tempted, I am tempted of God: for God cannot be tempted with evil, neither tempteth he any man: But every man is tempted, when he is drawn away of his own lust, and enticed. Then when lust hath conceived, it bringeth forth sin: and sin, when it is finished, bringeth forth death. Do not err, my beloved brethren. Every good gift and ev-**

**ery perfect gift is from above, and cometh
down from the Father of lights, with whom
is no variableness, neither shadow of turning.**" Jas. 1:13-17.

The word "temptation" in the above passage is translated
from the Greek "peirazo" and means, "to test, entice, discipline, prove, tempt or try." God doesn't <u>test</u> anybody with
evil, <u>entice</u> anybody with evil, <u>discipline</u> anybody with evil,
<u>prove</u> anything with evil, <u>tempt</u> anybody with evil or <u>try</u>
anybody with evil. Thus, God has no relationship <u>with</u> evil.
It is not in His nature. Evil <u>cannot</u> be traced back to God.
Moreover, this passage clearly says that evil <u>can</u> be traced
back to man. It is man who has an ongoing relationship with
evil, not God. It is man's "own lust" which draws his heart
away <u>from</u> God <u>to</u> Satan's spirit, which then "conceives" and
gives birth to "sin" and "death." Remember, Satan is the one
Scriptures call "the Tempter" (Matt. 4:3), not God.

Jesus taught us that when evil "tares" are sown among good
"wheat," that it is <u>not</u> God who does it but rather, "An enemy
hath done this." (Matt. 13:24-28). The Apostle John com-
mented very clearly that God's purpose was not <u>with</u> evil
but <u>against</u> it. **"He that committeth sin is of the devil; for
the devil sinneth from the beginning. For this purpose
the Son of God was manifested, that he might destroy
the works of the devil."** 1 Jn. 3:8. Jesus came to destroy the
evil works of Satan by overcoming them with the Father's
goodness. **"How God anointed Jesus of Nazareth with the
Holy Ghost and with power: who went about doing good,
and healing all that were oppressed of the devil; for God
was with him."** Acts 10:38. Satan comes to **"steal, and to
kill, and to destroy"** but Jesus came that we **"might have**

life" and **"have it more abundantly."** Jn. 10:10.

Jesus' major point to us was to show that His Heavenly Father was <u>always</u> and <u>only</u> good. No Old Testament saint knew God as "Abba," an Aramaic term used by Jesus as a title for His Heavenly Father which essentially means "Daddy." Jesus came to reflect the Father's love which never gives His sons "serpents" or "stones" or "scorpions," but instead freely gives His sons "bread" and "fishes" and "eggs" and most importantly "the Holy Spirit." (Lk. 11:11-13). This passage says that if earthly fathers **"being evil, know how to give good gifts unto your children: how much more shall your Heavenly Father give"** us all things for life and godliness. This is the same Father to whom James refers to in the following passage: **"Don't be deceived, my dear brothers. Every good and perfect gift is from above, coming down from the Father of the Heavenly lights, who does not change like shifting shadows."** Jas. 1:16-17.

James strongly warns us to, "LET NO ONE SAY" God is related to evil in any way, and "DO NOT ERR, MY BELOVED BRETHREN" by saying that anything <u>other</u> than good and perfection "ever" cometh down from the Father of light (Jas. 1:13,16). This was the message of the Gospel - - God hasn't, doesn't and won't allow evil. **"This then is the message which we have heard of him, and declare unto you, that God is light, and in him is no darkness at all."** 1 Jn 1:5.

In God's eyes, evil has never been something to "allow," but rather is a malignancy which must be "overcome." **"Be not overcome of evil, but overcome evil with good."** Rom. 12:21. What's radically different about God is that He always overcomes evil with the power of perfect goodness. God the Father is this way (Matt. 5:44-45,48), God the Son is this way (Acts 10:38), and so must we be this way as the body of Christ (Rom. 12:21). **"Be ye therefore perfect, even as your Father which is in Heaven is perfect."** Matt. 5:48.

Point Two: Jesus Is God's Total Disallowance of Evil

God's only view toward evil is to disallow it <u>through</u> the life, death and resurrection of His Son Jesus Christ. This is the power of the Cross - - to conquer and nullify evil in all its forms - - sin, sickness, death, wrath, violence, hatred, jealousy, strife, pride, lust and envy. John the Baptist was the first to recognize and declare Jesus' mission as the cure for all the world's evil.

> **"The next day John seeth Jesus coming unto him, and saith, Behold the Lamb of God, which taketh away the sin of the world."** Jn. 1:29.

The term "taketh away" in the above passage really means "beareth away." At the Cross, Jesus bore away all the power of evil in our lives - - past, present and future - - bar none - - no exceptions. There is no sin, or evil or demonic power that the Cross of Jesus did not overcome. Jesus said, "be of good cheer; I have overcome the world." (Jn. 16:33).

Don't lose this point. Sometimes, we can miss the most crucial point by neglecting to focus on it with our whole being. Jesus came to destroy evil, and He did destroy it. **"He that committeth sin is of the devil; for the devil sinneth from the beginning. For this purpose the Son of God was manifested, that he might destroy the works of the devil."** 1 Jn. 3:8. Why evil still appears to exist and prosper is a question soon to be answered. But for now, know that the Scriptures declare that Jesus is God's full provision to prevent, protect and purify us from evil. Jesus described His own purpose as follows:

> **"The Spirit of the Lord is upon me, because he hath anointed me to preach the Gospel to the poor; he hath sent me to heal the brokenhearted, to preach deliverance to the captives, and recovering of sight to the blind, to set at liberty them that are bruised, To preach the acceptable year of the Lord."**
> Lk. 4:18-19.

Jesus came to heal the brokenhearted - - from evil, to preach deliverance to those held captive - - by evil, to restore the sight of those blinded - - by evil, and to set at liberty those that are bruised - - by evil. Jesus' heart is always to bless and protect us. **"Behold, I give unto you power to tread on serpents and scorpions, and over all the power of the enemy: and nothing shall by any means hurt you."** Lk. 10:19.

Jesus never tolerated, used or allowed evil in any form. He defeated what is called "natural evil" when He rebuked a storm which threatened to sink the boat in which He was traveling. He defeated "demonic evil" hundreds, if not thousands, of times by casting out spirits of infirmity, insanity and deformity. He protected an adulteress from "social evil" by keeping her from being murdered by other men. He battled "religious evil" constantly as He rebuked the false religion of His day which blocked people from entering the gate of truth. He overcame the "material evil" of lack by multiplying loaves, transforming water into wine and finding needed finances in the mouth of a fish. Lastly, Jesus defeated the "ultimate evil" by raising others and Himself from the dead. HE CONQUERED DEATH!

Whenever Jesus was not allowed to save others from evil, He marveled at their unbelief which kept them from receiving deliverance (Mk. 6:1-6). When He instructed the disciples to pray "this way," the heart of Jesus' prayer was His statement in the Greek imperative that His Heavenly Father does and will "deliver us from evil."

I hope these verses will help lift Jesus up in all our eyes as God's ultimate gift to vanquish all evil. God gave His all to us. Never ask again, "Why does God allow evil?" He doesn't. To believe He does ignores, dishonors and maligns the blood, work, sacrifice and wonderful name of Jesus.

Now, the question might be asked that if at this very moment I have an evil thought or commit an evil act, hasn't God "allowed" me to think evil or do evil? Couldn't He force me by controlling my thoughts or body to not commit evil? The answer is no. It is not in God's nature to coerce, manipulate or force another. God does woo us, help us, convince us, and even rebuke us. But God never coerces and forces us. Just as it is impossible for God to lie, it is impossible for God to use coercion. I know this is a challenge to conventional thinking, but it is the only way God's goodness as revealed in the previous Scriptures listed in this chapter can be true and consistent.

The prefix "omni" means "all." God is omnipotent (all-powerful), omniscient (all-knowing), but God is not omni-causative. He doesn't <u>cause</u> or even <u>allow</u> everything to happen 24/7. God does not put His necessary "stamp of approval" on evil acts before they are allowed to occur. If He does, then He is responsible for evil. We seem to think that God in some sense allows murder since He doesn't strike the murderer down with lightning right before the murder is committed. Does God have the power to strike down murderers before they act? I say no because God's power is defined by His character and nature. God certainly has the power to hide, protect and deliver the righteous from harm, but He won't and can't use violence to stop violence. Jesus was repeatedly delivered away from stonings, but He never used violence on the aggressors, even taking the time on one occasion to heal the severed ear of one of His attackers (Lk. 4:29-30; Jn. 7:30, 44; 8:59; 10:31,39; Lk. 22:50-51).

God will not and cannot act outside of His good and true nature. For instance, if God cannot lie (Tit. 1:2), can God claim to be all-powerful if there is something He is unable to do? Well, this depends on how you define all-powerful. If all-powerful means God can do anything at anytime, then God is not all-powerful because He can't and won't lie - - ever. Yet, if all-powerful means that He has unlimited power within the context of His perfect character and true nature, then God is certainly all-powerful in that regard. He only operates in all-powerful truth, never in all-powerful lies; in all-powerful love, never in all-powerful violence; in all-powerful tenderness, never in all-powerful cruelty; in all-powerful patience, never in all-powerful wrath.

This is easy to see in the context of lying, but what about other attributes which are not in His divine nature? What if killing is not in God's nature? What if mental coercion is not in God's nature? What if physical coercion is not in God's nature? What if manipulation, revenge, pettiness, brutality, cruelty and frustration are all not in His nature? Then, it is just as "impossible" for Him to act out of these motives as it is for Him to lie. The point is that being all-powerful <u>and</u> all-good means that God's power operates <u>only</u> within the context of His character. God never acts or operates "outside of" or "inconsistent with" His perfect goodness, which is His agape nature of love described in 1 Corinthians 13. As St. Francis de Sales said, *"Nothing is so strong as gentleness. Nothing is so gentle as real strength."*

Thus, God won't lie to us, kill us, coerce us, manipulate us, brutalize us, abuse us, threaten us or terrorize us. God will protect us, bless us, correct us, teach us, convince us, strengthen us, encourage us and deliver us. Consider the following passage from Saint Anselm:

> *How can you be omnipotent, O God, if you cannot do all things? How can you do all things if you cannot sin - - if you cannot lie, if you cannot make false what is true? If you are unable to sin, you cannot claim to be able to do all things. Or is it that sin stems not from power, but from powerlessness? For those who commit sin have so little power over their own natures that they actually harm themselves. They are at the mercy of forces which they cannot oppose . . . .*
>
> *The more people have power to commit sin, the more they are powerless. So, Lord God, you are in fact more truly omnipotent because you cannot act through powerlessness.*
>
> *Proslogion, Chapter 7.*

Why would God use tactics He commands us not to use?
Why would He tell us not to kill, hate, hurt or avenge ourselves on our enemies, while He treats His own enemies with
wrath, vengeance, brutality and destruction? Or, put another
way, why would God tell us to overcome all evil with good,
unless He Himself did the exact same thing? *"God forces no
one, for love cannot compel, and God's service, therefore, is
a thing of perfect freedom."* Hans Denk. Isn't this clear from
reading the following verses?

> **"Ye have heard that it hath been said, An
> eye for an eye, and a tooth for a tooth: But
> I say unto you, That ye resist not evil: but
> whosoever shall smite thee on thy right
> cheek, turn to him the other also. And if any
> man will sue thee at the law, and take away
> thy coat, let him have thy cloke also. And
> whosoever shall compel thee to go a mile,
> go with him twain. Give to him that asketh
> thee, and from him that would borrow of
> thee turn not thou away. Ye have heard
> that it hath been said, Thou shalt love thy
> neighbour, and hate thine enemy. But I say
> unto you, Love your enemies, bless them
> that curse you, do good to them that hate
> you, and pray for them which despitefully
> use you, and persecute you; That ye may
> be the children of your Father which is in
> Heaven: for he maketh his sun to rise on
> the evil and on the good, and sendeth rain
> on the just and on the unjust. For if ye love
> them which love you, what reward have
> ye? do not even the publicans the same?**

> And if ye salute your brethren only, what
> do ye more than others? do not even the
> publicans so? Be ye therefore perfect, even
> as your Father which is in Heaven is per-
> fect." Matt. 5:38-48.

Since we are to be perfect <u>as</u> our Heavenly Father is perfect
in overcoming evil with good, then this brings the need for
the great missing element in this discussion - - "patience."
God is able to overcome <u>all</u> evil by patiently enduring and
bearing all our evil until we repent. If God weren't patient,
then we would all be dead or writhing in Hell right now.
If God weren't patient, He would use force, violence, coercion and wrath to work His will. If God weren't patient, then
the Cross would not exist to deliver us from <u>all</u> evil. God's
agape love **"thinketh no evil; Rejoiceth not in iniquity,
but rejoiceth in the truth; Beareth all things, believeth
all things, hopeth all things, endureth all things."** 1 Cor.
13:5-7. <u>This</u> is God's nature, always enabled by supernatural
"patience," which in the original Greek literally means "joyful endurance." God's "mercy [joyfully] endureth forever"
(Ezra 3:11). We are likewise called to patience:

> **"My brethren, count it all joy when ye fall
> into divers temptations; Knowing this, that
> the trying of your faith worketh patience.
> But let patience have her perfect work,
> that ye may be perfect and entire, wanting
> nothing."** Jas. 1:2-4.

To know this type of patience is to know God and to share
in His sufferings. **"That I may know him, and the power
of his resurrection, and the fellowship of his sufferings"**

Phil. 3:10. We "joyfully endure" because we are walking in the resurrection power of God, but we also suffer as we mourn the world's ongoing rejection of Jesus. Yet, we know that the world will one day be overcome with God's goodness and reconciled to the love of God. Our faith and patience will help hasten the Day of the Lord while our sinful impatience and unrighteous wrath will delay it.

The point is that God does not allow evil. He <u>disallows</u> it through the "faith <u>and</u> patience" of Jesus Christ (Gal. 2:20; Heb. 6:12-20). Understanding <u>how</u> God overcomes evil now gives us the wisdom to know in what sense He hasn't, doesn't and won't <u>allow</u> evil. The next revelation is to understand that God has <u>already</u> disallowed all evil.

Point Three: God Has Already Disallowed All Evil

We need to remember that Hebrews 4:1-10 says that God has already rested from His works. Actually, the Lord's works were fully and finally completed prior to the seventh day of creation. This is possible due to His power of "determinate counsel and foreknowledge" (Acts 2:23). Before Adam fully digested the poison apple, God had already predestined the coming of Christ as our full cure for <u>all</u> forms of evil and death. This is why Jesus' work at the Cross was actually completed from God's view "before the foundation of the world" (1 Pet. 1:20; Heb. 4:3). This is why Jesus is described as "the Lamb slain from the foundation of the world" (Rev. 13:8). This is why Christians' names were "written in the book of life from the foundation of the world" (Rev. 17:8). From God's perspective, He has always already completed His works of salvation toward any and all situations - - past, present or future.

God's works are <u>always</u> complete and <u>already</u> accomplished. Always already! Compare it to a shining star at night. The star's actual image shining through our darkness may be thousands or millions of years old (the star itself may in fact no longer exist), but the image is providing us current and active light to penetrate our darkness. The ancient image of the star has always already completed its work long ago, yet its brightness shines across time and space to illuminate all our "nows."

So too, God's light in Jesus Christ was complete ages ago at His Cross and Resurrection, yet His light shines on our darkness across all time and space. The light of His life is complete and fully accomplished. Yet it still shines currently on us as if it just happened.

To carry the analogy further, a star's light shining on us <u>offers</u> us light that we can still refuse to receive. I can hide under a blanket, in a closet or just shut my eyes. When I do this, I am <u>currently</u> rejecting and blocking a fully completed and accomplished source of light. Here, the rejection of the light is not based on the inadequacy of the light, but rather is based on my unwillingness to receive it.

Think about the enormity of this truth. If God has always already disallowed <u>every</u> form of evil, then we are left with a stunning conclusion - - <u>we</u> are the ones who <u>allow</u> evil by our blocking God's disallowance of it by our individual or corporate unbelief. Or, put another way, we have the freedom to accept or reject God's disallowance of evil. God's disallowance of evil is the Cross of Christ. The more we accept the completed work of the Cross, the more we accept God's disallowance of the evil we face. The more we neglect or ignore the completed work of the Cross, the more we reject God's disallowance of evil.

Let's establish the Scriptural basis for the proposition that God has always already disallowed every form of evil. First, Jesus has already defeated every demonic power and disarmed every demonic weapon which has ever plagued mankind. Jesus "led [past tense] captivity captive" through His death, resurrection and ascension (Eph. 4:8). Theologians call this the "Harrowing of Hell," whereby Jesus led a prison-break to set us free from all demonic oppression and captivity. **"And having spoiled principalities and powers, he [Jesus] made a shew of them openly, triumphing over them in it."** Col. 2:15. Greek scholars describe this verse as detailing a victory parade where Jesus displayed all the demonic armor and weaponry stripped off of the enemy through His Cross and Resurrection two thousand years ago. Jesus is not going to do this - - He already has done it. All demonic power has already been long ago defeated, long ago disarmed and long ago dispossessed of all evil influence. All evil is now bound by the blood of Jesus. John Bunyan, in his classic *Pilgrim's Progress*, envisioned Satan's power as lions chained on both sides of life's highway. As long as Christian, the hero of the book, stayed on the straight and narrow path, the lions could not touch him. Only if he removed himself from the safe path back into the areas where the lions were bound could they then harm him. God has already bound all demonic power for those who walk with and in Christ. It can only harm us as we stray off and away from the Lord's path, which I like to call the Psalm 91 highway. Psalm 91 describes in detail the pure and absolute protection God provides true believers.

It gets even better. Not only has the demonic been demolished, but we have also already been completely healed of all our sins, sorrows and sicknesses. Jesus again completed this healing long ago through His Cross and Resurrection: **"Who his own self bare our sins in his own body on the tree, that we, being dead to sins, should live unto righteousness: by whose stripes ye <u>were</u> healed."** 1 Pet. 2:24. The Old Testament prophesied that Jesus would heal us in the <u>future</u> "with His stripes" (Is. 53:5). The Gospels declared that Jesus' earthly ministry was currently healing us <u>then</u>: **"When the even was come, they brought unto him many that were possessed with devils: and he cast out the spirits with his word, and healed all that were sick: That it might be fulfilled which was spoken by Esaias the prophet, saying, Himself took our infirmities, and bare our sicknesses."** Matt. 8:16-17. Lastly, the epistle of First Peter, written decades later, stresses that the work of Jesus' Cross and Resurrection was then final and complete, "by whose stripes ye <u>were</u> healed." (1 Pet. 2:24). Deuteronomy lists sickness, death, weakness, oppression, poverty, strife, depression, war, violence and broken relationships all as the curses of the law which afflict fallen man. Yet, "Christ <u>has</u> redeemed us from the curse of the law." Gal. 3:13. Do you see? Were and has. We <u>were</u> healed because He <u>has</u> fully redeemed us from all evil.

If demons are defeated and all our sins and sicknesses healed, then why don't we see this "always already" victory right now?

> **"How shall we escape, if we neglect so great salvation; which at the first began to be spoken by the Lord, and was confirmed**

**unto us by them that heard him; . . . Thou
hast put all things in subjection under his
feet. For in that he put all in subjection under him, he left nothing that is not put under him. But now we see not yet all things
put under him. But we see Jesus, who was
made a little lower than the angels for the
suffering of death, crowned with glory and
honour; that he by the grace of God should
taste death for every man." Heb. 2:3, 8-9.**

This passage is clear that <u>all</u> things have already been put
under Jesus, but we don't yet see them put under Jesus. The
reason? Because of our individual and corporate "neglect"
of "so great a salvation." Hans Denk eloquently described
this ruling dynamic of "neglect" which runs rampant in fall-
en man: *"O my God, how does it happen in this poor old
world that Thou art so great and yet nobody finds Thee, that
Thou callest so loudly and nobody hears Thee, that Thou art
so near and nobody feels Thee, and Thou givest Thyself to
everybody and nobody knows Thy name? Men flee from Thee
and say they cannot find Thee; they turn their backs and say
they cannot see Thee; they stop their ears and say they cannot hear Thee."* Both Satan and Evil have no gasoline left
in their tank because Jesus drained it all away at the Cross.
They are functioning today solely off the fumes of our neglect of Jesus' great salvation. What makes this salvation so
great is its "always already" aspect. The ministry of the Holy
Spirit is to convince us of the accomplished benefits of this
great salvation. **"Now we have received, not the spirit of
the world, but the spirit which is of God; that we might
know the things that are freely given to us of God."** 1 Cor.
2:12. Consider the following passage which likewise con-

firms that <u>all</u> things have <u>already</u> been put under Jesus' feet:

> **"That the God of our Lord Jesus Christ, the Father of glory, may give unto you the spirit of wisdom and revelation in the knowledge of him: The eyes of your understanding being enlightened; that ye may know what is the hope of his calling, and what the riches of the glory of his inheritance in the saints, and what is the exceeding greatness of his power to us-ward who believe, according to the working of his mighty power, Which he wrought in Christ, when he raised him from the dead, and set him at his own right hand in the Heavenly places, Far above all principality, and power, and might, and dominion, and every name that is named, not only in this world, but also in that which is to come: and hath put all things under his feet, and gave him to be the head over all things to the church, Which is his body, the fullness of him that filleth all in all."** Eph. 1:17-23.

Let's not be like Israel and Ephraim whom God had already delivered from oppression "but they knew not" and were "bent to backsliding" (Hos. 11:3,7). In other words, they neglected their so great a salvation and were taken captive. Instead, let's be like those four intrepid lepers in 2 Kings 7 who dared to leave the besieged gates of Samaria. Rather than waiting in fear and starvation to die with the rest of the city, they dared to enter into the camp of the enemy Syrians. There they discovered that God had already caused the enemy to scatter and flee leaving behind all their food, treasures, supplies, cattle and weapons. The lepers then gorged themselves on food and treasure. Then they went back to proclaim to all Israel that the enemy had already been disarmed and defeated and that Israel was victorious because the Lord Himself delivered them. Israel's fear of a non-existent enemy kept them imprisoned and oppressed. So too with us. Our fear of a totally defanged devil keeps us in needless famine and weakness. Let's always be quick out of the gate to see this great truth - - Jesus has always already defeated every demonic enemy.

It is crucial to understand the difference between God's omni-presence and His manifest presence. God has always already conquered all evil. His victorious omni-presence continually and steadfastly announces the once-and-for-all victory of Christ. Yet, mankind largely ignores God's omni-presence. But, whenever a man, through the hearing of faith, recognizes and realizes Christ's past victory over the present situation, then God's omni-presence manifests the reality of that victory to this visible world - - right now! Until a man receives by faith God's omni-present victory, then that victory will not manifest in the visible world. Our faith, then, is just the valve that opens and releases God's omni-presence unto manifestation.

Let me give you an analogy. Imagine that I take a flashlight, turn it on, and place it against my stomach with the light aimed up at illuminating my face. Now, imagine that I put a thick towel over the bulb. The light is now present but not manifest to the visible eye. Even though certain wavelengths of light may be passing through the towel and shining on my face, these wavelengths aren't perceptible to the naked eye.

Even though light is burning bright and is ready, willing and able to illuminate my countenance, I have draped darkness over it to keep it from visibly manifesting.

Jesus is always the light of the world, ever ready and willing to shine healing on all. Yet, when He went back to Nazareth, He could do no mighty work because they had draped a towel of unbelief over Jesus' presence which kept them from recognizing and realizing the omni-present and omni-available healing presence of God. And Jesus marvelled at their unbelief (Mk. 6:1-6). Had any of them just heard by faith the omni-present victory of God, then they could have received God's omni-presence unto visible manifestation.

When you consider the work of Jesus, focus on it as a flashlight already completely turned on and aimed at your life. He is not going to turn His light on and toward you in the future. He always already has His salvation light turned on and toward you. All we must do is to never neglect this so great a salvation. Our neglect drapes towels of unbelief over situations and keeps God's works in the omni-present unseen rather than the manifest seen. To this day there remains a veil (towel) over many men's eyes which keeps them from recognizing the light of the Messiah to save them in all their ways. The veil (towel) is done away in Christ (2 Cor. 3:15-18). As the mind is renewed, the veils (towels) are removed and the light of Christ shines forth (Rom. 12:1-2).

Remember, we are now sons of God (1 Jn. 3:2), but we have not yet fully manifested as sons of God (Rom. 8:19). Hebrews 2 tells us that all is in subjection to Jesus now, but that we don't now see that subjection. Do you see? There is a fully completed omni-present subjection of all evil to Christ, but that subjection will not <u>manifest</u> until men recognize, realize and release it by faith unto <u>this</u> realm. We will become <u>manifest</u> sons of God when we allow God's presence to <u>manifest</u> in this realm. God has done His part - - fully. He now awaits a generation of Christians who will do their part, in <u>fully</u> recognizing and realizing the completed work of Christ. May it be us!

Beloved, do you see why we must never accuse God of allowing evil? He has given His own blood, sweat and tears to disallow evil in every form. Acts 2:22-24 tells us that Jesus was delivered to us in "the determinate purpose and foreknowledge of God" in order to defeat death and evil - - and Jesus <u>did</u> (past tense) defeat death and <u>all</u> Satanic oppression once and for all (Acts 10:38; 1 Jn. 3:8). The only reason evil appears to be alive and well is due to our own neglect of God's great salvation which has always already provided us deliverance from all evil. God, through His foreknowledge and unsurpassable power, has <u>already</u> pre-responded to every encounter with evil appearances which we will ever have, and He has predestined and pre-fixed a way of escape from every apparent threat of evil.

> **"And we know that all things work together for good to them that love God, to them who are the called according to his purpose. For whom he did foreknow, he also did predestinate to be conformed to the image of his Son, that he might be the firstborn among many brethren."** Rom. 8:28-29.

> **"There hath no temptation taken you but**

**such as is common to man: but God is faith-
ful, who will not suffer you to be tempted
above that ye are able; but will with the
temptation also make a way to escape, that
ye may be able to bear it."** 1 Cor. 10:13.

Again, always already. Jesus tells us that whatever we bind
on Earth has "already" been bound in Heaven. The original Greek of Matthew 18:18 and 16:19 both clearly say that
we have the authority to bind on Earth that which is already
bound in Heaven. Interlinear translations agree that these
verses convey the idea that, "whatever you might bind on the
Earth will <u>be</u>, having <u>been</u> bound in the Heavens already."

This is why Jesus used the Greek imperative mood when
teaching us "how to pray" in Luke 11:1-4. The imperative
mood doesn't ask, beg or cajole God. The imperative mood
<u>orders</u> reality to conform to God's already established will.
Jesus isn't asking God the Father to deliver us from evil in
this passage. Jesus is <u>ordering</u> all reality to be conformed to
His Father's always already complete deliverance from evil.
Consider John 15:7 which states, "If ye abide in me, and my
Words abide in you, ye shall <u>ask</u> what ye will, and it shall be
done unto you." The Greek word translated as "ask" in this
passage is defined in *Strong's* Concordance at 154 and 4441
as "strictly a demand of something due."

When Jesus told his disciples, "Let your loins be girded"
(Lk. 12:35), He used the perfect imperative, which literally
meant, "Let your loins be in a state of already having been
girded." Likewise, Jesus used the perfect imperative to rebuke the elements on the lake of Galilee (Mk. 4:39) where
He in essence commanded the storm, "Be in a state of hav-

ing already been rendered harmless." Jesus' imperatives here were based on the always already completed works of His Father. Jesus merely punctuated the events into final manifestation here in the visible world of what already existed in Heaven.

In other words, the imperative mood merely <u>orders</u> our immediate sphere of influence to conform to the already completed work of the Cross. We don't pray <u>toward</u> God to complete His promises. Rather we pray <u>from</u> God's already established and completed work. Our prayer is a form of worship and release where we say yes and amen to all the promises of God which have already been fully performed by our magnificent Savior. Beloved, God has already rested from all of His works of deliverance, and so must we. **"There remaineth therefore a rest to the people of God. For he that is entered into his rest, he also hath ceased from his own works, as God did from his. Let us labour therefore to enter into that rest, lest any man fall after the same example of unbelief."** Heb. 4:9-11.

Do you see this magnificent reality of God's salvation? Always already. Always already. God's salvation is always already. This view of God changes everything. No longer is prayer seen as a laborious effort to get God to act or "change His mind." Prayer is now seen <u>not</u> as a way to change God's will, but rather as a way of <u>implementing</u> God's will - - His "always already" will to all goodness. As Paul Bilheimer said, prayer is not overcoming reluctance in God to save us, but rather prayer is overcoming our own reluctance to believe God's willingness to save us to the uttermost. Worship is not based on what God might do someday, but rather true worship rejoices in what God has already fully accomplished.

All we need do is to rest in the completed work of the Cross. Sure, there may be suffering. Sure, there may be temptation. Sure, there may be persecution. Sure, there may be occasional stumbles and a few set-backs. But in all these things, we are more than conquerors <u>because</u> Jesus has always already pre-conquered all these problems. Blaming God for allowing these problems is like blaming the fireman who pulls us out of a fire for starting the fire itself. God didn't start the fire - - we did. God gave His own blood to rescue us from the fire of sin with which we have burned ourselves.

The blood of Jesus is much mentioned and much preached. But, one crucial aspect of the blood is neglected - - it <u>was</u> shed two thousand years ago. It is a past accomplished fact that Jesus' blood once and forever disallows and cleanses all evil within us and outside us. Like the shining star at night mentioned previously, Jesus' blood shines <u>from</u> two thousand years ago <u>to</u> "now." While many today still close their eyes to this light, thus blocking God's disallowance of evil, the body of Christ must learn to keep its eyes open to the "always already" Kingdom of light. The major way we keep the eyes of our hearts open is to <u>not</u> <u>err</u> as a beloved brother-in-Christ by letting ourselves or anyone else say that God allows evil and that <u>anything</u> other than good and perfection <u>ever</u> comes from Him (Jas. 1:13,16). This mindset ignites and oxygenates *The Jesus Mood* to burn bright and non-stop.

Chapter 3
Duality: Mother of all Mood Killers

B efore we look at what Duality <u>is</u>, let's first look at what it's <u>like</u>. Duality is like the Spanish throwing weapon known as the "bolas." This weapon consists of two weighted balls tied on both ends of long interconnected cords. The weapon is hurled in a spinning motion which causes the cords to entangle around the limbs of the victim. The weighted balls continue to cause the straps to entwine around the victim until the balls themselves knock the victim senseless.

Duality is Satan's bolas. He hurls mindsets at us weighted with two contrasting fixed principles. Once this bolas wraps around our mind, it begins to constrict and bind our thinking until one or both of the twirling concepts knocks us spiritually senseless. This leaves us in confusion and without the imperative faith of *The Jesus Mood*. The result is that we are left in a perpetual state of double-mindedness which renders us unstable in all our ways and unable to receive anything from God (Jas. 1:6-8).

What is Duality? It is Satan's primary weapon of deception. Learning to avoid the snares and bolas of Duality will keep you safe and secure in *The Jesus Mood*. Duality is what robs us of certainty in God. Oswald Chambers said that the origin of all sin is found in the mistrust of God's character. Mistrust starts with Duality and ends with uncertainty.

So just what exactly is Duality? How is it rooted in the mistrust of God's nature? How does Duality keep us tripped up and trapped in the uncertain moods of *maybe\might\if* and away from the imperative mood of Jesus? Why is Duality a mood killer?

The dictionary definition of Duality is any mindset which is ruled and regulated between two supreme principles. Before the birth of Christ, Persia and Greece were both infested with dualistic religion and philosophy. Their two ruling principles varied depending upon the particular group. Some saw the two supreme principles as "good and evil," others as "light and darkness," and still others as "spirit and matter" or "body and soul." The Gnostic heretics of the first century were ruled by the dualism of spirit and matter. They believed all matter was evil and temporary and that all spirit was good and eternal. They either became haters of the material world by becoming ascetic monks or they became hedonists who pleasured themselves materially because they felt it had no eternal consequence. All of their perceptions and judgments hinged on this dualistic mindset.

Racism is fiercely dualistic, where one race is ruled by the two concepts of "my race" and "everyone else." Under this tragic mindset, the racist pigeonholes all virtues to his kind and all vices to the other kind. Most people, without realizing it, process all things on a sliding scale between two opposite but connected concepts.

I once had an epiphany about beauty. I was listening to a group of people single out certain school girls as the "beautiful ones." I felt the grieving of the Holy Spirit in my belly as other so-called "plain girls" were being ignored. In a moment in time, I saw that in the Lord's eyes all girls were beautiful - - bar none. I realized my grieving came from the fact that the beautiful girls were defined by not being the plain girls. Conversely, the plain girls were defined by not being beautiful. In other words, the Duality of beauty and ugliness was ruling these people. For every girl whose beauty they singled out, there was a silent accusation that another girl not singled out was not beautiful. Under this mindset, "judging" someone as beautiful necessarily "condemns" someone as ugly.

I knew the Lord's heart was similar to the lyrics of an old Ray Stevens song, *"Everything is beautiful in its own way."* I repented and purposed that instead of singling out beautiful girls, I was going to single out the beauty in all girls. There would be no more ugly duckling Duality judgments in my life. Now, whenever I behold someone who strikes me as beautiful, I purpose to look for and declare the unique beauty of all others nearby. Nothing is wrong with singling out beauty, but when we do it dualistically it puts callouses on our hearts and eyes which prevent us from seeing other forms of unique and varied beauty.

I had a similar insight about competitive sports. While I was watching my seven year old son play soccer, I noticed something amazing. All the boys on the field were grim faced - - some crying in frustration, others pouting and still others intensely panicked about their performance. On the sideline, in sharp contrast, the second-stringers were playing soccer up against the fence - - no referees, no coaches and no grim looks. Instead, the boys were having a ball. Laughing, rollicking, yet still giving their best effort. These boys were not enslaved to the dualistic mindset of win or lose. They were living the adventure of life to the full right then and there! The one thing of "wholeheartedness" was their defining motive, not the two things of winning or losing. **"And whatsoever ye do, do it heartily, as to the Lord, and not unto men."** Col. 3:23.

I grew up as the most competitive person imaginable. I was miserable whenever I lost at anything. Happiness came only from winning. It didn't matter the contest - - board games, card games, football games, wrestling matches - - I had to win. My poor sportsmanship is legendary. I yelled at wrestling referees, basketball referees and even mock trial judges at law school. Losing at anything was death to me. On one of my early dates with my wife, she beat me at tennis. My romantic response? I picked up the empty tennis official's stand and hurled it several feet into the air. Praise God nobody ever got hurt. Praise God my wife could see past my hot-headed sickness and continue to date me.

I share all this to say that I know the mindset of those miserable boys on the soccer field all too well. I was well into my thirties before this sickness was broken. I can honestly say the need to win doesn't enslave me any longer. The only thing that matters is doing whatever I do as unto the Lord and not unto man. It's not about winning, it's about loving. When we live by the hearing of faith, sometimes we will "appear" to lose to further the love of God. This is what martyrdom is all about.

On a much simpler level, I have taught my seven children that winning is not the main thing. When we play football or basketball, we will play to tie and not to win. The only rules we go by are to <u>never</u> give up and <u>always</u> encourage each other. Usually, love's best lets the losing side catch up and tie or even win. Often, we don't even keep score but keep totally focused on giving our best effort. In other words, we have fun without anyone having to be labeled "the loser."

The mindset of Duality stabs the arrows of misery, aggression, jealousy and strife into the heart of all competitive events. Winners under this cruel Duality are defined as non-losers. Losers are defined as non-winners. Duality always defines one thing in terms of the other. However, the soccer game on the sideline didn't have <u>two</u> ruling dynamics, but only <u>one</u> - - life! The Lord our God is one, not two. God is life, not Duality. The life of God in Christ Jesus is <u>one</u> thing that covers everything, not <u>two</u> things that cover everything. Since nothing can compare to God's supreme oneness, then all twoness wrongly elevates man-made divisions and distinctions. The Hebrew mindset views God as incomparable with any other person, place or thing. Nothing is to be compared or contrasted with Him. He is matchless, peerless and transcendent. **"I, even I, am the LORD; and beside me there is no saviour. . . .Thus saith the LORD the King of Israel, and his redeemer the LORD of hosts; I am the first, and I am the last; and beside me there is no God. . . .I am the LORD, and there is none else, there is no God beside**

**me: I girded thee, though thou hast not known me. . . .
Remember the former things of old: for I am God, and
there is none else; I am God, and there is none like me."**
Is. 43:11; 44:6; 45:5; 46:9.

The Shema

"Hear O Israel, the Lord is our God, the Lord is one." Deut.
6:4. This verse is the first line of the Shema, which is the
basic statement of Jewish faith and is prayed daily by all
observant Jews. Christians likewise place great importance
on this verse as a declaration of the "oneness of God." To
recite this verse in faith is to declare that our <u>everything</u> is
ruled by <u>one</u> <u>thing</u> - - the Kingdom of God. Even though as
Christians we heartily believe in the Holy Trinity, we still af-
firm the oneness of God. Father, Son and Holy Spirit are described as three-in-<u>one</u>, three Persons in <u>one</u> Godhead, three
distinct identities but <u>one</u> essence. Thus, both Christians and
Jews emphasize the oneness of God as a foundational belief.
**"There is one body, and one Spirit, even as ye are called
in one hope of your calling; One Lord, one faith, one baptism, One God and Father of all, who is above all, and
through all, and in you all."** Eph. 4:4-6.

What does Deuteronomy 6:4 mean when it says that we are
to "hear" that "the Lord is one?" To "hear" is to perceive. We
are to perceive God's "oneness" in all things. It is not just
mentally knowing God is one. It is hearing it and hearing it
and hearing it. Christians are to have a "single-eye" toward
the oneness of God. **"The light of the body is the eye: if
therefore thine eye be single, thy whole body shall be full
of light. But if thine eye be evil, thy whole body shall be
full of darkness. If therefore the light that is in thee be**

darkness, how great is that darkness! No man can serve two masters: for either he will hate the one, and love the other; or else he will hold to the one, and despise the other. Ye cannot serve God and mammon." Matt. 6:22-24.

The above passage highlights that "single-eyed" devotion to God cannot serve "two masters." The oneness of God speaks to our "sole" vision of a "sole" God reigning in "sole" authority and power over our lives. Whenever God is not our "sole" source, then demonic Duality is corrupting and defiling our spiritual walk.

Let me give you an illustration. Right now, lift your left hand up above your head as far as you can reach. Let's imagine that this hand represents God's "sole" reign over your life - - His oneness. In other words, God is above, over and greater than anything else - - any other person, event, idea, opinion, sickness, threat, oppression or circumstance (Is. 55:8-9). Nothing <u>can</u> be compared or contrasted to God. Nothing <u>is</u> to be compared or contrasted to God.

Now, what fallen man always does is to lift up our right hand above our head and keep it next to our left hand. We take some event, person or thing and raise it in importance to either compare or contrast it with God. Now there are two things, two masters to serve, two ideas to grapple with, two alternatives to debate, two options to choose, two poles to slide between, two moods to vacillate between. This is the Duality which wears our faith down and eventually kills it.

Man was not created to serve two masters, only "one." God's ways, thoughts and actions are higher and better than our ways. We are not to compare or contrast earthly ways, thoughts and actions with God's Kingdom. To compare or contrast is to bring natural thinking to supernatural existence. It won't work. It only results in dualistic pride, shame or blame. There is a Hebrew name for God, "Ein-Sof," which is translated "The Infinite." This speaks to the transcendent nature of God above and beyond all earthly concepts. When we stop trying to define God, instead posturing ourselves under His oneness, then God will rule and reign within us in "sole" dominion - - without doubt, Duality and death.

New Testament Scripture dispenses all Duality. In Christ there is no Jew or Greek, male or female, slave or free, circumcised or uncircumcised (Gal. 3:26-29; 1 Cor. 7:17-24). In Christ, these dualistic distinctions don't exist. Whenever distinctions like these are maintained, divisions, strife, judgment and pride follow. Chaos is the result.

Think back and consider Adam and Eve in the Garden of Eden. There were two trees of consequence - - the *Tree of Life* and the *Tree of the Knowledge of Good and Evil*. Death was the consequence of the *Tree of the Knowledge of Good and Evil*. Eternal life was the consequence of the *Tree of Life* (Gen. 2:16-17; 3:22).

Notice anything? The death tree has two ruling principles - - good and evil. The life tree has one ruling principle - - eternal life. The Duality of the Knowledge of Good and Evil kills us, while the single-principled *Tree of Life* gives eternal life. There is an old saying which I have only recently grasped, "Behold but one in all things; it is the second that leads you astray." As the great Christian mystic Meister Eckhart explained, "We must learn to penetrate all things and find God there."

Before the fall, Adam could only see God in all things. This is what allowed him to name all living creatures and to walk

with God in the cool of the Garden. Adam was so aware
of seeing one in all things, the one being God, that he was
not even aware of the Duality of being clothed or naked. He
wasn't aware of being "over" or "under" dressed because he
was dressed "in God." He was too focused on the oneness
of the Creator which he beheld in all creation. Adam didn't
have to self-consciously plan and choose his day's activities
before the fall. Rather, Adam naturally fulfilled God's purposes spontaneously without the curse of self-consciousness,
self-determination, self-doubt and self-righteousness.

But Satan had a plan. Step by step, Satan led Adam and Eve
toward a mine field of Duality. There were five distinct and
deadly mines which Satan lured Adam and Eve to detonate
in the Garden of Eden. Let's lay a foundation on these five
types of Duality and see where in the Garden they first ex-
ploded into our world.

The Five Types of Duality

Duality is as simple as *"This **and** That."* Duality always divides. Sometimes it divides into the violent opposition of *This*
versus *That*. Sometimes it divides our life into an endless ar-
ray of self-willed choosing of *This **or** That*. Sometimes it divides into works-based living where all that we desire must
be earned or manipulated through our own effort of *This **for**
That*. Still other times, Duality divides our thinking into continual judgments as we arrogantly assign blame or credit for
all events before us - - *This **from** That*. Lastly, Duality can
divide by blending together two opposites into a false yin\
yang unity that is not of God - - *This **and** That*. The *Tree of
the Knowledge of Good and Evil* is really the Tree of *This\
That* Mindsets.

Duality #1: *This versus That*

The first type of Duality we will look at is *This* **versus** *That*. This is radical dualism which sets up two poles of existence with no room for compromise between. This Duality is what starts wars, hate, strife, competition, racism, fundamentalism, terrorism and aggression. Force is the prominent dynamic here. This mindset sees all life as battle. There is only winning and losing, fighting and overcoming, attacking and surrendering.

The problem with this mindset is not just "what" it thinks but "how" it thinks. There is no rest, unity or abiding joy because like the cold-blooded shark, we must continually swim or die in the waters of force and conflict. Everyone who is not on my side is an enemy to be subdued, converted or conquered. Other men are dehumanized into pawns with whom I must either compete or challenge. Us *versus* them. This is how Hitler recruited young men. He would have them turn in a family member for sedition. This act cemented the youth's allegiance to Hitler's "us" *versus* the "them" of the rest of the world. It is no different for any recruiting sect, whether it's religious, military or social. They all seek to foster allegiance to some *This* **versus** *That*.

The tragedy of this mindset is that it uses man-made distinctions to keep men's teeth sharpened toward one another. Our default setting toward one another is suspicion, resentment and aloofness. This mindset lives in the valley of peril - - usually either threatening or feeling threatened.

Under this form of Duality, it's always an eye for an eye and a tooth for a tooth. It's winning at all costs. It's attacking at all provocation. It's the alpha male. The caveman. The mercenary. The business shark. The competitive athlete whose greatest joy is defeating opponents. It is Napolean, Alexander the Great and Machiavelli.

But, aren't we to oppose evil? Isn't winning better than losing? Aren't we to use our best effort to prevail in all things? We are certainly to oppose evil, but <u>not</u> dualistically (Matt. 5:38-48). We are called to be <u>more</u> than dualistic winners - - much more (Rom. 8:37). We are not to use our best effort to dualistically conquer the world, but rather we are to strive to enter into the Sabbath rest of God where He has <u>already</u> conquered the world with the love and life of Christ (Heb. 4:1-11).

The Duality of *This **versus** That* says if our eye or tooth is struck, then we must strike back at the eye or tooth of the attacker. Force for force. Blow for blow. But Jesus said, "resist not evil; but whosoever shall smite thee on thy right cheek, turn to him the other also" (Matt. 5:39). What a Duality-breaker! Good overcomes evil not by opposing it on its own terms of force, violence and competition. Rather, good overcomes evil by allowing itself to be victimized <u>without</u> striking back. This makes us "perfect" just as our "Father which is in Heaven is perfect" (Matt. 5:48).

Romans 8:37 is often quoted for the purpose of conquering our enemies. But read the text carefully: **"Who shall separate us from the love of Christ? shall tribulation, or distress, or persecution, or famine, or nakedness, or peril, or sword? As it is written, For thy sake we are killed all the day long; we are accounted as sheep for the slaughter. Nay, in all these things we are more than conquerors through him that loved us. For I am persuaded, that neither death, nor life, nor angels, nor principalities,**

nor powers, nor things present, nor things to come, Nor
height, nor depth, nor any other creature, shall be able
to separate us from the love of God, which is in Christ
Jesus our Lord." Rom. 8:35-39. The victory in this passage
refers to staying in the love of Christ by not allowing the trials of life to separate us from God. The conflict then is not
about conquering our enemies with force, but rather about
abiding in the continual agape-love of God. Abiding in His
love doesn't make us dualistic conquerors. Instead, it makes
us "more" (better, greater, truer) than any conqueror could
ever be.

Just what is it that needs conquering anyway? As outlined in
Chapter Two, Christ has always already overcome, forgiven
and reconciled the world to Himself. He did this by absorb-
ing all the venom of our sin-nature into Himself at the Cross.
He did this without any retaliation or wrath toward His attackers. In this non-dualistic act of "resisting not evil," He
conquered the world with forgiveness and love. Our calling
is to realize and recognize Jesus' completed victory and then
to rest in it with our whole being. **"There remaineth therefore a rest to the people of God. For he that is entered
into his rest, he also hath ceased from his own works, as
God did from his. Let us labour therefore to enter into
that rest."** Heb. 4:9-11.

The Sabbath rest is merely resting in the always already accomplished work of the Cross. No more competing. No more
challenging. No more fighting. No more violence - - verbal,
physical or mental. In their place will abide the peace of *The
Jesus Mood* which transcends all Duality. Like the majestic
eagle which is able to use its mighty wings to fly above and
beyond all storm clouds, so too are we able to fly on eagle's

wings above all the Duality clouds of *This\That* uncertainty into the high Heaven of imperative faith. Theologians call this Christus Victor - - Christ already victorious over all the powers of evil!

Duality #2: *This or That*

The second type of Duality we will look at is *This **or** That*. What we have in our fallen state is freedom <u>of</u> choice. What we crave as Christians is freedom <u>from</u> choice. We want pure, simple and natural obedience to the Holy Spirit's direction for all things. **"For as many as are led by the Spirit of God, these are the sons of God."** Rom. 8:14.

Choice itself is the problem. The fundamental problem is not <u>what</u> we choose, but <u>that</u> we choose. To live by our own choices is cursed self-righteousness. To live in the Spirit is to live by God's righteousness. Again, choice is the root problem. We choose and choose and choose and choose and choose - - choosing ourselves to death in the process. This is what cursed self-righteousness is - - taking it upon ourselves to "choose" our own way <u>as</u> God (Gen. 3:5). Adam fell into death when he started living by the "choosing of good and evil" instead of by the "hearing of faith" (Gal. 3:2,5).

William Law said it best: "Our own will separates us from God. Or, rather, our own will is separation from God." Do you see? We were not created to choose between *This **or** That*. We were created to obey love's call. The love of God is to continually constrain and compel us at all times. The Greek word for "choose" is "hairesis" and is translated in the New Testament as "heresy," which is a label synonymous with spiritual error (Gal. 5:20; 2 Pet. 2:1). Choosing from among alternatives is earthly, sensual and demonic (Jas.

3:15). Allowing the Holy Spirit in us to resolve all our decisions (Phil. 2:13) is the wisdom from above which is pure, peaceable, gentle, willing to yield, full of mercy and good fruits, without partiality and without hypocrisy (Jas. 3:17). Count me in!

But aren't we supposed to learn Bible precepts so that we can know what conduct to choose in our lives? No! The Apostle Paul knew Bible precepts up and down and front and back. Yet, in Romans 7, Paul tells us "choosing" will never work righteousness - - never. **"For we know that the law is spiritual: but I am carnal, sold under sin. For that which I do I allow not: for what I would, that do I not; but what I hate, that do I. If then I do that which I would not, I consent unto the law that it is good. Now then it is no more I that do it, but sin that dwelleth in me. For I know that in me (that is, in my flesh,) dwelleth no good thing: for to will is present with me; but how to perform that which is good I find not. For the good that I would I do not: but the evil which I would not, that I do. Now if I do that I would not, it is no more I that do it, but sin that dwelleth in me. I find then a law, that, when I would do good, evil is present with me. For I delight in the law of God after the inward man: But I see another law in my members, warring against the law of my mind, and bringing me into captivity to the law of sin which is in my members. O wretched man that I am! who shall deliver me from the body of this death? I thank God through Jesus Christ our Lord. So then with the mind I myself serve the law of God; but with the flesh the law of sin." Rom. 7:14-25.**

Paul's power of choice brought him death and failure. "Choosing" is a Satanic snare that keeps us from the "hearing of faith." In the Spirit, there is nothing to choose, only unctions to obey. In "choosing" there are always "two" things, whereas in the hearing of faith there is only "one" thing - - obedience. But, isn't the decision to obey a choice? No, I want to draw a distinction between decisions and choices. Choices, as I am using the word, are *"This or That"* selections between two <u>external</u> options based on natural reasoning and understanding. Decisions, on the other hand, are <u>internal</u> resolutions to yield to the Holy Spirit's prompting and guidance. The Holy Spirit may illuminate reasons in giving us understanding about the dynamics involved in the decision, but the decision itself is not reason-based. It may be reason-enhanced, but never reason-based. As Meister Eckhart said, "The just man has no reason for doing what he does." This is because the just man is led by the Spirit of God, a Spirit which is above, beyond and greater than <u>any</u> reason-based precept. The wisdom of God seems foolish to man. The wisdom of man <u>is</u> foolish to God. In fact, the foolishness of God is wiser than the wisdom of men. For man, to live by choice is to live by foolishness. When we renounce "choice," we are enabled to clearly receive urgings, promptings and resolutions from the Holy Spirit. In other words, renounce "choice" and you will hear God's "voice," the voice of the Holy Spirit leading you in all your ways.

I have seven children. Sometimes, it feels like I am running a small country. When I get trapped in Duality, I often feel relentless <u>pressure</u> to choose, choose and choose. It wears me down and out and I end up mentally paralyzed, depressed and self-condemning about what I have wrongly chosen, what I am not choosing or about what I need to choose. However, when I am strong in the Holy Spirit, I don't think in terms of choice. The Holy Spirit leads me by unction - - an inner knowing and sure prompting. I feel no pressure, no condemnation, no Romans 7 angst. Instead, I flow in peace, joy and goodness. I am able to be completely present in the moment, ready and available for God's love to move me.

Whenever self-awareness grips me, self-doubt and self-condemnation follow - - I have just entered the Romans 7 "zone." The good news is that Romans 8 is nearby, ready to save me from all condemnation through the life of the Spirit. Romans 8 tells me that in Christ there is no condemnation (v.1), no sin (v.2), no death (v.2), no carnal mindedness (v.6), and no defeat (v.37). In Christ, there is only life (v.2), righteousness (v.4), spiritual mindedness (v.6), peace (v.6), physical quickenings (v.11), continual leading by the Holy Spirit (v.14), Abba intimacy (v.15), Holy Spirit witness (v.16), Holy Spirit strengthening (v.26) and the inseparable love of Christ (v.35-39).

Am I saying reason, choice and logic play no part in everyday life? Of course not. Reason has a supporting role but not the starring role. Walking in the Spirit, the hearing of faith, the life of God in Christ Jesus - - the star of this glorious stage is not reason but love. Love trumps reason. It illogically leaves the ninety-nine to go after the one.

Rene Descartes (1596-1650), the father of modern philosophy and science, believed in nothing that scientific reason could not empirically prove. Descartes believed that his ability to reason and doubt justified and proved his own existence. His self-consciousness and ability to make dualistic choices is that on which he based his whole system of philosophy. Reason, doubt and the ability to choose form this unholy trinity of spiritless living.

In his own words, Descartes' analysis was, "to accept nothing as true which I did not clearly recognize to be so, and to reject as absolutely false everything as to which I could imagine the least ground of doubt." This attitude, called "Cartesian Doubt," rejects everything the mind is unable to fully prove by scientific method. Daniel Boorstin, in his book *The Seekers*, writes that Descartes by, "starting with doubt as the catalyst of his philosophy he makes the doubter the center of his universe." Boorstin concludes that Descartes' motto "I think, therefore I am," is better described as, "I doubt, therefore I am." How similar this attitude is to that of doubting Thomas: **"But Thomas, one of the twelve, called Didymus, was not with them when Jesus came. The other disciples therefore said unto him, We have seen the Lord. But he said unto them, Except I shall see in his hands the print of the nails, and put my finger into the print of the nails, and thrust my hand into his side, I will not believe."** Jn. 20:24-25.

Descartes discounted all miracles, mysteries and supernatural experiences because the mind of man can't prove them by reason. What Descartes changed with one fell philosophical swoop was both the object and source of man's faith. The object of man's faith is no longer God but man's own intellect and ability to choose and doubt. Man's way of dualistically thinking becomes his own god. The source of man's faith is no longer the heart, but the mind. Man only believes what he can intellectually prove to himself. Thus, Descartes removed both God from the center and faith from the heart. In their place, man was put in the center while faith was dualistically exiled, dissected and mutated into the realm of *"This or That"* intellect. Now, dualistic choice was king. To be or not to be. To believe or not to believe. To choose *This or That*.

The Apostle Paul started from a fallen place of radical Duality where "choosing" circumcision <u>or</u> uncircumcision meant everything, "choosing" to eat kosher <u>or</u> unkosher meant everything and "choosing" to obey <u>or</u> not obey every jot and tittle of the law meant everything. However, hallelujah, Paul ended in a place of divine oneness where "choosing" circumcision <u>or</u> uncircumcision means <u>nothing</u> (1 Cor. 7:19), "choosing" to eat clean <u>or</u> unclean means <u>nothing</u> (Rom. 14:14; 1 Cor. 6:12) and "choosing" to obey <u>or</u> not obey every jot and tittle of the Old Testament law means nothing (Gal. 2:21-3:25). Finally, Paul dispels all Duality in the following passage: **"For ye are all the children of God by faith in Christ Jesus. For as many of you as have been baptized into Christ have put on Christ. There is neither Jew nor Greek, there is neither bond nor free, there is neither male nor female: for ye are all one in Christ Jesus. And if ye be Christ's, then are ye Abraham's seed, and heirs according to the promise."** Gal. 3:26-29. Paul finally saw that the problem wasn't <u>what</u> we choose, but <u>that</u> we choose. We don't choose God. We allow ourselves to be chosen of God. We don't choose God. We yield to His decisions already formulated in us and for us. We don't choose God. We "lassen" Him. Lassen is a German word used by philosopher Martin Heidegger to describe the spiritual act of "letting and releasing" as opposed to the carnal act of "taking and using." Martin Luther and the Anabaptists used this term to describe the theology for a "letting loose" of one's self unto God in an attitude of total dependence, humility and trust. Whereas "choosing" wrongly attempts to seize the things of God, "lassening" rightly seeks to yield to the Spirit of God in all our ways.

Duality #3: *This for That*

The third type of Duality we will consider is *This for That*. This is the curse of "works righteousness" where we try to make things happen with our own efforts. What "this" must I perform to get the "that" I want? How do I "earn" the blessing and love of God? How do I "earn" the blessing and love of men?

This for That Duality is ruled by the Latin term "quid pro quo," which essentially means "something for something" or "one thing in return for another." Our first thought toward any desired goal is usually, "What must I <u>do</u> to obtain the desired result?"

This form of Duality is trapped in causality. How can I <u>cause</u> my desires to be accomplished? The "law" became cursed when men started viewing it as a way to <u>cause</u> God's favor. Men wrongly use the law as a means to accomplish an end. In contrast, God uses the end to allow the means. Galatians and Romans clearly teach us "the law" kills us when we view obedience to it as the cause of our righteousness. Rather, God gives us the end result first, the life of our indwelling Christ, to then operate within us to <u>fulfill</u> the means of righteousness. Do you see this critical distinction? Duality says I cause my own righteousness by choosing to obey the law - - i.e. I <u>pay</u> the price of obedience. In contrast, true Christianity says Jesus Christ <u>is</u> my righteousness which now <u>allows</u> me to fulfill the law by the hearing of faith - - i.e. Jesus freely gives me His power to be obedient. Thus, true obedience is not the <u>cause</u> of spiritual power, but rather true obedience is the freely given <u>fruit</u> of spiritual power. This difference makes all the difference. The end (Jesus' life) produces the means (spiritual obedience), rather than the means (legal-istic\dualistic obedience) producing the end (right standing before God). Righteousness produces obedience, not vice versa.

This for That Duality is also the spirit of "Mammon" which sees all things as transactional. I must pay "this" for "that" to happen. This is what drives financial markets, govern-ments, political movements and social standing. Under this warped view, people are no more than bargaining chips to be used for private gain. All events and relationships are seen as potential assets we use to obtain our wants. We view each other as resources to accomplish a goal. This is why our re-lationships are so conditional and fragile. We discard others when they stop being an asset to our desires. How shallow. How petty. You can't interact with an asset in any meaning-ful way. You can't develop an unbreakable bond of love with an asset. You can only use an asset up to get something else you want.

Jesus said we can't serve God and Mammon. In other words, the Mammon based Duality of *This for That* doesn't work in the Kingdom of God. My heart breaks as I see people unable to receive the things of God because they serve Mammon with their greed or fear. Even though these people heartily agree with the truths of God, they can't abide in spiritual peace because strongholds of financial lust or financial wor-ry dominate their thoughts. These strongholds become stran-gle-holds which literally choke out the Word of God. Satan lured Adam and Eve with the apple of lack. Satan convinced them they were missing something big! God was keeping something from them - - power to be "as God." If they would only eat the fruit, Satan claimed, then this act would "cause" them to become gods. They bought the lie and attempted to "cause" their own destiny apart from God. The great downward spiral began and continues to this day.

The bottom line with *This for That* Duality is that it pressures us to continually "choose" and "cause" our own righteousness rather than "resting" in the righteousness and resolve of Christ. Whereas some famous philosophers like Aristotle and Leibniz argued for the supremacy of causality and choice, others like David Hume argued that no absolute certainty can ever exist with causality and choice.

Quantum physicists side with Hume's approach as they have discovered that causality is not king and that there is an inherent level of uncertainty and unpredictability which underlies all reality. In fact, Quantum Physics provides the ultimate Duality-breaker by proving that all things - - me, you, the furniture, an electron - - we are all simultaneously both a particle and a wave. This truth is impossible to a dualistic mindset which sees "particle" and "wave" as mutually exclusive terms. Duality doesn't work in Quantum Physics. Quantum Physics says that the Duality of insisting on knowing two things simultaneously makes certainty impossible, because the more accurately one member of the pair is known, the less accurately the other is known. Quantum Physics has proved that you cannot simultaneously know with certainty where an electron is (position) and where it is going (momentum). Moreover, the electron itself can't know where it is (position) and where it is going (momentum), not with certainty. The price for living in Duality is certainty. Duality, choice and causality are the doomed dynamics of the *Tree of the Knowledge of Good and Evil*. They may work temporarily, for a season, for a time. But, they cannot work eternally because they lack the certainty of *The Jesus Mood*. They rob us of the one and only thing we must have to walk with God - - certainty.

While the philosophers and physicists continue to duel about Duality, one thing is apparent. The eternal certainty of *The Jesus Mood* cannot be "caused" by the choices of men. We merely "lassen" (let and release) *The Jesus Mood* up, through and out of us. In the Kingdom of God, there is nothing to be chosen or caused, only eternal life to let and release.

Duality #4: *This from That*

The fourth type of Duality is *This from That*. This is the Duality that blames or boasts. It points the finger at what is and then assigns blame or credit. If something bad appears, the finger of blame condemns the selected source. If something good appears, then this Duality jumps in to take credit for it. This is the mindset that blameshifts, condemns, boasts, and self-justifies. Under this Duality, finger pointing is King: **"Then shalt thou call, and the LORD shall answer; thou shalt cry, and he shall say, Here I am. If thou take away from the midst of thee the yoke, the putting forth of the finger, and speaking vanity."** Is. 58:9.

The "putting forth of the finger, and speaking vanity" can refer to the finger of blaming or the finger of boasting. The finger of blaming is pointed at others. The finger of boasting is pointed at self. The finger of blaming says "I accuse." The finger of boasting says "I deserve." Satan used both these dynamics to lure Adam and Eve to the tree of deathly Duality. Satan pointed the finger of blame at God "accusing" the Lord of wrong motives in wanting to keep the man and woman ignorant and powerless (Gen. 3:1-7). Satan also lured

Adam and Eve to adopt the mindset that they "deserved better" than God's provision. Do you see? "I accuse" and "I deserve" form the root system of Duality. This root system spreads into our every thought and every emotion until we are slaves to selfishness, self-centeredness and self-rule. Self is enthroned as the judge of all things, endlessly "pointing the finger and speaking vanity."

Jesus taught that we are not to judge others for bad things nor are we to take credit for any good thing. **"Judge not, that ye be not judged. For with what judgment ye judge, ye shall be judged: and with what measure ye mete, it shall be measured to you again."** Matt. 7:1-2. **"So likewise ye, when ye shall have done all those things which are commanded you, say, We are unprofitable servants: we have done that which was our duty to do."** Lk. 17:10.

The blame game. The fame game. Gross over-simplification. Men blame each other for everything bad. Or, men usurp the credit for everything good. Adam and Eve sin. Eve blames the serpent (Gen. 3:13). Adam blames the woman <u>and</u> God - - "it was the <u>woman</u> <u>You</u> gave me" (Gen. 3:12). In the next chapter, their son Cain becomes crestfallen when he doesn't receive the credit he thinks he deserves from God (Gen. 4:5). His recourse? He blames his brother Abel - - and kills him (Gen. 4:8).

Do you see? *This from That* must accuse someone or something else for all misfortune. Blame-shifting. Blame-creating. It avoids personal responsibility by pointing the finger of blame elsewhere. Conversely, when credit for the good is at stake, this Duality jumps up to take the limelight.

Duality #5: *This and That*

False unity. False oneness. Demonic unity. Demonic oneness. Man-made unity. Man-made oneness. It's all the same. *This and That* is the Duality falsely disguised as oneness, which makes it the trickiest of all the Duality types. It claims it is not dualistic, but in truth it is the most dualistic of all. Instead of putting *This versus That*, choosing *This or That*, paying *This for That*, claiming *This from That*; *This and That* blends opposites together in a poisonous stew of "earthly, sensual, demonic" wisdom which produces confusion and every evil thing (Jas. 3:15-16). This false unity comes from the self-will and natural thinking of men enabled by demonic power.

This Duality is most easily seen in New Age spirituality which is pervasive in today's society. There are New Age gurus on every street corner, bookshelf, television station, and talk show. They all proclaim the same basic truths - - we are all one - - God is all and all is God - - all division is false - - we need just to embrace our oneness with all things and we will find our own divinity. This is what Gnosticism taught two thousand years ago and it is no different today. The New Age teaching is Gnosticism repackaged. Both operate in the deadly Duality of *This and That*.

But it's not just New Age. Eastern religion and philosophy both claim a false oneness which blends everything into one thing. Yin\Yang is the concept which falsely blends opposites like *good\evil, masculine\feminine, strength\yieldedness* and *rigidness\fluidity* all into one thing. These contrasting qualities become different sides of the same <u>one</u> coin. When we walk in "the way," or the "tao," of "yin\yang," or *This and That*, we realize that all things are both good <u>and</u> evil, masculine and feminine, strong and yielded, rigid and fluid. The "tao" blends all these contrasting qualities into "one" quality. We now seek to recognize the oneness of all things through their yin\yang aspects.

What is the problem with this? Is *New Age\Eastern\Gnostic* "oneness" the same as Christian "oneness?" No! Only in Christ do all things reconcile, cohere and have their true being (Col. 1:16-17). All other "oneness" is artificial, empty and lonely because it is devoid of the personality and centrality of Jesus. False oneness brings false peace, false wisdom and false spirituality.

When I see New Age gurus weaving their spells of "oneness" over gullible listeners, I see a glazed look come over the faces in the audience. They look serene, but only in the way a Hindu cow passively grazes and gazes its life away in an empty pasture.

God is a person. That person is Jesus. As a person, Jesus obviously has a personality. This personality now indwells all Christians. This personality is one personality - - and only one. It is a love personality. It is a hope personality. It is a faith personality. The personality of Jesus reveals the personality of the Heavenly Father. The Holy Spirit reveals the personality of Jesus. The body of Christ reveals the personality of the Holy Spirit. What oneness, what unity and what inter-dependence!

Contrast this with New Age views which claim that God is not a personality to relate with, but rather is a thing, an impersonal force with which we are to casually connect. *New Age\Eastern\Gnostic* thought is so barren and lonely. Whenever I have read or listened to their claims, I feel a profound sadness at the loneliness and isolation this false teaching produces. Their true fruit is not "oneness" but "aloneness."

Christian "oneness," on the other hand, produces intimate fellowship with the "otherness" of God. Even though we are called to be "one" with God in Christ, we are not called to be the same as God. This is at the heart of the matter - - New Age teaches you that you are God, I am God, we are God. They teach we are the same as God, the very same, the exact same. This outrageous claim is not true "oneness," it is true blasphemy.

Christian "oneness" teaches we have our being with God and in Christ, but does not teach we are the "same" as God, the "same" as Jesus or the "same" as the Holy Spirit. While we can live continually in full fellowship with and in the Godhead, we are not the Godhead. To reckon oneself the same as God takes away all interaction with God. If man is the same as God, he need only relate to and love himself. There is no "other" to relate with, to worship toward, to hear from, to go to, to lean on, or be comforted by. Self is all and all is self.

Don't embrace the dangerous Duality of *This **and** That*. Don't blend holy and unholy into a false oneness, a man-made oneness where we situate ourselves "as God." This was the snare in the Garden of Eden. Satan promised that by eating the fruit of the tree of Duality, the knowledge of good and evil, they would then exist "as God." What a lie! They became worshipers of "self" who could only hide behind fig leaves of blame, shame and fear. True repentance is yielding ourselves back to the true "oneness" of God, the sole Lordship of Christ, the New Testament Shema - - Hear O Christians, the Lord our God is ONE - - one faith, one hope, one baptism, one Lord, "One God and Father of all, who is above all, and through all, and in you all" (Eph. 4:4-6).

One final warning about the Duality of *This **and** That*. When we attribute light <u>and</u> darkness, good <u>and</u> evil, love <u>and</u> wrath to God's nature, we are dualistically blending things which must not be blended. God is <u>only</u> light. **"This then is the message which we have heard of him, and declare unto you, that God is light, and in him is no darkness at all."** 1 Jn. 1:5. We must not <u>blend</u> darkness into God's nature. Blending darkness with light causes Spiritual schizophrenia, which the Bible labels "double-mindedness." Let not this man expect to receive anything from the Lord (Jas. 1:6-8). Light and darkness do not mix - - at all. In Christ "is no darkness at all."

God is not evil. He is good, only good, always good. God has no connection to evil. **"Let no man say when he is tempted, I am tempted of God: for God cannot be tempted with evil, neither tempteth he any man: But every man is tempted, when he is drawn away of his own lust, and enticed. Then when lust hath conceived, it bringeth forth sin: and sin, when it is finished, bringeth forth death. Do not err, my beloved brethren. Every good gift and every perfect gift is from above, and cometh down from the Father of lights, with whom is no variableness, neither shadow of turning."** Jas. 1:13-17. This most precise passage on this point instructs us to "Let no man say" God has any connection with evil. It also admonishes us "Do not err" by saying that anything <u>other</u> than good and perfection ever comes from God.

"God is love." 1 Jn. 4:8. Jesus came not to judge the world with wrath, but to save the world with love (Jn. 12:47). Scriptures don't say God <u>is</u> wrath, but that God <u>is</u> love. Jesus was God's message to mankind of **"Glory to God in the highest, and on earth peace, good will toward men."** Lk. 2:14. Wrath is <u>our</u> rejection of God - - our <u>own</u> neglect of our so great a salvation. Wrath is the place <u>we</u> give to Satan through sin, hardness of heart and unbelief. Wrath is <u>not</u> God, nor is wrath from God, of God or by God. Wrath is man-generated, Satan-dominated and fear-perpetuated. Jesus is the cure for this wrath, not the cause of it. Never blend love <u>and</u> wrath into God's nature. Never blend good <u>and</u> evil into God's nature. Never blend light <u>and</u> dark into God's nature.

The word "blend" often reveals dualistic thinking because it still views things in terms of two. It just seeks to artificially mix the two so that they will appear as one. Rather than blending all things together as they are, we are to purify our hearts and minds before the throne of God. All impure thoughts and emotions are not to be "blended" but "transcended." All that is impure is to be removed, not by battling wickedness on its own dualistic terms, but rather by cleaving to the precious Jesus in all our ways. **"Therefore thus saith the LORD, If thou return, then will I bring thee again, and thou shalt stand before me: and if thou take forth the precious from the vile, thou shalt be as my mouth."** Jer. 15:19.

The Conclusion of the Matter

All our bad moods come from Duality. *This **versus** That* leaves us violent, competitive and angry. *This **or** That* leaves us continually focused on choosing between external appearances rather than yielding to the inner leading of the Spirit. *This **for** That* leaves us trapped in works-based living where we must <u>cause</u> our own destiny. *This from That* leaves us endlessly blaming or bragging about current conditions. Lastly, *This **and** That* tries to artificially blend all things into one stew, a stew which is ultimately poisoned with demonic deception and Godless living.

As I said in the opening paragraph of this chapter, Duality is like the Spanish throwing weapon known as the "bolas." This weapon consists of two weighted balls tied on both ends of long inter-connected cords. The weapon is hurled in a spinning motion which causes the cords to entangle around the limbs of the victim. The weighted balls continue to cause the straps to entwine around the victim until the balls them-selves knock the victim senseless. Satan, likewise, hurls mindsets at us weighted with two supreme fixed principles of *This\That*. These mindsets wrap around our thoughts and begin to bind our thinking until one or both of the twirling concepts knocks us spiritually senseless. We must learn to "duck" when bolas of Duality are hurled at us. Understand-ing the five forms of *This\That* Duality will allow us to de-velop quicker spiritual reflexes to duck away from danger.

These five forms of Duality rob us of faith, certainty, peace, love and uninhibited interaction with God. *The Jesus Mood* transcends all dualistic notions of *This\That* by abiding in the "always already" Kingdom of Heaven. In this blessed spiritual stratosphere, we are no longer enslaved to violence, choice, Mammon, blame or self. We are free to live by the "hearing of faith." Faith comes by hearing God. Hearing comes from a listening heart-interaction with the Holy Spir-it. This is the faith we are to live by, the faith we are to grow in, and the faith we are to pass on to others.

The purpose of understanding these five forms of Duality is to help us better recognize and take captive our own toxic mindsets which hinder our walk with God. Duality snares are always just a thought away, so we must train ourselves to be ever vigilant in our thought life. Island spotters in the Pacific during World War II would have a chart of enemy airplane shapes which they would refer to when planes were seen passing overhead. If the shape in the sky matched the shape on the chart, then the spotter would radio that an enemy plane had been spotted. Learning these five types of Duality will also allow us to chart enemy mindsets as they seek to fly overhead in our own thought life. Once spotted, we can act decisively to confer with the Holy Spirit and take them captive to the obedience of Christ. **"For though we walk in the flesh, we do not war after the flesh: (For the weapons of our warfare are not carnal, but mighty through God to the pulling down of strong holds;) Casting down imaginations, and every high thing that exalteth itself against the knowledge of God, and bringing into captivity every thought to the obedience of Christ; and having in a readiness to revenge all disobedience, when your obedience is fulfilled."** 2 Cor. 10:3-6.

When Duality is broken, we are free to hear God's undistorted wisdom for our lives. When Paul saw that <u>in</u> Christ there was no Jew or Greek, male or female, bond or slave, he was then free to see all men as children of God (Gal. 3:28). When Paul saw that <u>in</u> Christ neither circumcision nor uncircumcision availed <u>anything</u>, he was set free to become a new creation (Gal. 6:15). When Paul saw that <u>in</u> Christ clean and unclean foods were <u>both</u> acceptable if eaten in faith, he was set free to enjoy the fruits of all creation (Rom. 14).

The *mental\emotional\physical* violence of *This **versus** That* is broken by turning the other cheek and blessing our enemies. The pressure to externally choose *This **or** That* is broken by maintaining a single eye to stay yielded to the inner leading of the Holy Spirit. The works-based manipulation of *This **for** That* is broken by the recognition that God has "always already" provided us all things for life and godliness and that we are to abide in the Sabbath rest of God. The finger pointing accusations of *This **from** That* are broken by "judging not" and by "boasting not." Lastly, the forced blending of holy and vile by *This **and** That* is broken by cleaving only to the precious purposes of God in and for all things.

On a personal level, "Duality-breakers" have continued to bless and liberate my thinking. I recently discovered that someone I considered a friend of mine had been speaking vicious lies about me behind my back. My dualistic flesh wanted to fight (*This **versus** That*). I wanted my name vindicated and his name condemned. I knew this was coming from Duality and not from God. As I waited on the Lord, all I could hear the Lord lead me to do was confess over and over again, "The Lord is my shield. The Lord is my shield. The Lord is my shield!" I did. He was. The venom for vengeance left my body and I have nothing but pity and goodwill toward the person in question. I was able to forgive him because he didn't know what he was doing. Nobody who sins really knows what they are doing. I too often don't even know what I am doing - - except when I am yielding to the Holy Spirit's inner promptings.

On another recent occasion, my wife and I were presented with two apparent choices regarding one of our children's lives. We struggled not to analyze the situation as a *This **or***

That choice. I failed. My wife succeeded. As the deadline approached, I reasoned out the choice my flesh reckoned was the most logical. When I informed my wife what I decided, she lovingly disagreed and said she didn't have peace about my "choice." Twenty-four hours before the deadline, my wife heard from the Lord what the path of blessing was and we obeyed. I knew she was right. She had stayed out of Duality and not walked by sight. The Lord will direct our paths in and for all things if we will acknowledge Him in all our ways and wait for His leading. **"Trust in the LORD with all thine heart; and lean not unto thine own understanding. In all thy ways acknowledge him, and he shall direct thy paths."** Prov. 3:5-6. Don't be anxious. God's answer will bloom before your eyes. His answer will present itself.

My greatest daily challenge from Duality comes in the *This from That* area. My flesh cries out daily to blame, blame, blame. When I was younger, I tended to boast, boast, boast. The older I have become, the less I boast but the more I blame. However, they both are just as dualistically disgusting. It is so easy to point the finger at the drop of a hat. However, over the last few years, I have experienced great deliverance in this area. Through the revelation of PLENITUDE, a dynamic to be explored in the next chapter, I am eliminating the blame game from my thought life. The following verse has worked powerfully to renew my mind: **"Finally, brethren, whatsoever things are true, whatsoever things are honest, whatsoever things are just, whatsoever things are pure, whatsoever things are lovely, whatsoever things are of good report; if there be any virtue, and if there be any praise, I will continually think on these things."** Phil. 4:8.

I shared earlier in the chapter about my struggles in *This or*

That Duality where the pressure of "choosing" has in the past paralyzed me in condemnation, particularly in the area of parenting. However, this Duality type is also threatening in the area of finances where pressure to "choose" to spend or not to spend can strangle out all hope from the heart. Only the peace of God can save us here. **"Casting all your care upon him; for he careth for you."** 1 Pet. 5:7.

Lastly, some years ago the New Age Duality of *This **and** That* attacked very close to home. I read some New Age books and they poisoned me. Thankfully, the Lord did a quick work to reveal the deception and allow me to repent. These books sought to lead me away from the centrality and preeminence of Christ, replacing them with the centrality and preeminence of men. The New Age spirituality of men is vile and cannot, must not, and will not blend with the New Creation in Christ Jesus.

One of the Hebrew words translated in the Bible as "wait" means to gather together and twist into one bundle. When we wait upon the Lord, what we are really doing is purging out Duality by gathering up all things before us and tying them up into one bundle for the Lord. He is the Lord of all, one Lord over all, through all and in all. When we, as spiritual eagles, fly above the storm clouds of Duality, we will know peace, certainty and joy beyond understanding. God's ways are higher, better, stronger and truer than our ways. His ways are Duality-free. His way is the *Tree of Life*. Our fallen way stems from the dualistic *Tree of the Knowledge of Good and Evil*. Our Duality trees can and must be uprooted by the Spirit of God.

There is a term used to describe the difficulty in avoiding Duality - - "sitting on the razor's edge." Duality is a mental razor which is always just a thought away waiting to cut and divide anything into two things. But, by the Spirit of God, we are able to "hover" above the Duality razor and stay single-eyed on the one voice of God toward every situation. Nicolaus of Cusa (1401-1464) was one of the great German Christian theologians and thinkers. He wrote on Philosophy, Theology, Mathematics and Astronomy. More importantly, he was the first Christian thinker to understand and write extensively about the dangers of Duality. He wrote frequently about the Christian's need to "hover" above Duality by cleaving to the transcendent oneness of God. Nicolaus was convinced that this way of thinking was the only mindset compatible with true Christianity. Only this mindset can allow us to fully "rest" in the completed works of God.

Cleave to the oneness of God. Remember, behold but one in all things, it is the second that leads you astray. We must learn to penetrate all things and find Jesus there - - His purpose, His love, His willingness, His readiness, His ability, His provision, His authority, His Heavenly Father, His Holy Spirit - - this Jesus, **"Who is the image of the invisible God, the firstborn of every creature: For by him were all things created, that are in heaven, and that are in earth, visible and invisible, whether they be thrones, or dominions, or principalities, or powers: all things were created by him, and for him: and he is before all things, and by him all things consist. And he is the head of the body, the church: who is the beginning, the firstborn from the dead; that in all things he might have the preeminence."** Col. 1:15-18. Jesus' wonderful mood inhabits the Earth right now, waiting to be released into each and every situation of our lives, into each and every corner of our souls, and into each and every pore of our skin. Hallelujah!

Chapter 4
Plenitude

"**P**lenitude" is my favorite word. It comes from a Latin word meaning "fullness." It is the quality or state of being which is whole and complete. It is abundance. It is fulfillment. It is where potential is fully realized. Nothing remains undone or incomplete. It is present perfection which is ready, willing and able to fully manifest now. It is a cup currently running over. In other words, Plenitude is *The Jesus Mood.*

For the Christian, Plenitude is the spiritual dynamic that hears God promise "all things are yours" (1 Cor. 3:21-22). This is the mentality which is "rich toward God" (Lk. 12:21). Plenitude is not about greed to acquire spiritual riches, but rather is about praise and gratitude for "the riches of His grace" already bestowed on us in Christ Jesus (Eph. 2:7). "All things for life and godliness" have already been given to us by

God's "divine power" through "the exceeding great and precious promises" of Scripture which have made us "partakers of the divine nature" (2 Pet. 1:3-5). The Apostle Paul tells us again and again how very rich we are: "we <u>have</u> obtained an inheritance," and that the Father "<u>has</u> blessed us with <u>all</u> spiritual blessings in heavenly places in Christ," and that we need our eyes "enlightened" that we may "know what is the hope of our calling, and what the riches of the glory of his inheritance in the saints, and what is the exceeding greatness of His power toward us who believe, according to the working of His mighty power, which He <u>wrought</u> in Christ . . . and <u>has</u> raised us up together, and has made us sit together in heavenly places in Christ Jesus" (Eph. 1:11,3,18-20; 2:6). Do you see the "tenses" in all these promises? "Have" and "has." We are already rich in all things - - we just need to grow in the realization of it. Plenitude <u>is</u> that realization - - an ever-increasing recognition and appreciation of <u>who</u> we are <u>in</u> Christ and <u>what</u> we have <u>in</u> Christ.

Most importantly, Plenitude is a mindset. It is the mindset which <u>allows</u> *The Jesus Mood* to manifest. The suffix "tude" often attaches itself to words which refer to mindsets, such as atti<u>tude</u> and certi<u>tude</u>. "Attitude" is best defined as "a mood-setting mindset." A blessed attitude enables a blessed mood. An unblessed attitude enables an unblessed mood. "Certitude" is best defined as "freedom from doubt." Certitude is a completely convinced attitude. The crucial question then, is how can we develop and grow an attitude of certitude in and toward God?

The mindset of Plenitude will produce the attitude of certitude. Plenitude is a "mood-setting mindset" which produces the "freedom from doubt" which can only be found in the imperative mood of Jesus. As our attitude cleaves to the dynamic of Plenitude, then certitude will spread into every fiber of our being. Like the mustard seed, certitude will grow and grow until it dwarfs every other challenge of our lives. The certitude of Plenitude will shoot out branches of protection and deliverance for all our thoughts and emotions to safely abide under (Mk. 4:30-32).

Even though right now certitude may "seem" far from you, remember the mustard seed. It started off smaller than all else, but then grew larger than all else. It grows big, it grows non-stop and it grows fast (Mk. 4:26-32). The certitude of Plenitude is also like blessed leaven which began as just a measure but spread until "the whole lump was leavened" (Matt. 13:33).

The seed parables all describe the Kingdom of Heaven's growth <u>within</u> us as both quick and humongous. But what exactly is the Kingdom of Heaven? It is the attitude of Plenitude which births the certitude of Christ. It is freedom <u>from</u> doubt and freedom <u>toward</u> faith - - imperative faith which "worketh by love" in believing all things, hoping all things, and enduring all things - - faith which <u>never</u> fails (Gal. 5:6; 1 Cor. 13:7).

Beware Lackitude!

My least favorite word is "Lackitude." Actually, this word is not in any dictionary. I made it up to describe the fallen attitude of man which keeps us in servitude to the spirit of the world. "Servitude" is defined as "mental submission or slavery." The attitude of Lackitude produces servitude. Here, we unknowingly become prisoners of our own poor perspective about life, God and love.

So what exactly is Lackitude? If the Duality discussed in the last chapter is the cause of faithless moods, then Lackitude is the mood itself. Lackitude is the mental and emotional state of unbelief. Lackitude is the doubting disease. We view all things through the lens of doubt, discouragement, desperation and discontentment.

Under the feverish influence of Lackitude, we grumble, complain and murmur our lives away. When we look at our children, we too easily see what's wrong instead of what's right with them. Our view of our spouse is too easily corrupted with hard-hearted neglect. Parents are too easily viewed by children with ingratitude and dishonor. Siblings are too easily viewed as rivals. Friends are too easily viewed as disposable. Our jobs are too easily viewed as torture chambers to escape rather than callings to embrace. Resentment and angst dominate our moods.

Lackitude always wants to be somewhere else with somebody else doing something else. It is never content in the "now." Lackitude is the ruling dynamic of Hell. Hell says never enough - - never good enough, never full enough, never long enough and never true enough. **"Hell and destruction are never full; so the eyes of man are never satisfied."** Prov. 27:20.

Lackitude is the attitude of "lack." Like a moth to a flame, our mindset of lack draws us <u>to</u> the flames of sin and away <u>from</u> the life of faith. Lackitude focuses on God's absence rather than God's presence, on what God hasn't done instead of what God has always already done. Lackitude requires us to cast our confidence in God away. Repentance allows us to regain our confidence in God. All sin is really, at its root, is the casting away of our confidence in God in the present moment. **"Cast not away therefore your confidence, which hath great recompence of reward."** Heb. 10:35. The very next verse tells us that we "have need of patience" to receive the promises of God.

Lackitude starts where impatience begins. The virtue of patience will lead us to the promised land of Plenitude. The definition of the Greek word translated "patience" in the New Testament literally means "joyful endurance." It is "through faith and patience" (joyful endurance) that we "inherit the promises" of God unto manifestation (Heb. 6:12). We are to "count it all joy" while we steadfastly resist temptations of Lackitude, knowing that "the trying of our faith worketh patience" (joyful endurance) which is the "perfect work" of Plenitude and leaves us "lacking nothing" (Jas. 1:2-4). Jesus promised that in our patience we will possess our souls and He meant it (Lk. 21:19). Patience protects our souls from Lackitude and servitude.

Faith and patience is our way of cleaving to the Plenitude of God. The best news is that the indwelling Holy Spirit even helps us to do this from within our own hearts. **"For it is God which worketh in you both to will and to do of his good pleasure."** Phil. 2:13. The Holy Spirit continually bears witness with our spirits that we are children of God and joint-heirs with Christ (Rom. 8:16-17). The Holy Spirit is continually "convincing" us from within of sin, righteousness and judgment (Jn. 16:7-11). This passage says that sin is "believing not" on Jesus. Righteousness is believing <u>on</u> Jesus. Judgment is that the prince of this fallen world, Satan, is <u>already</u> defeated and judged. Beloved, consider this. The role of the Holy Spirit is to continually convince you from within of these three great truths - - all sin is unbelief <u>toward</u> Jesus, all righteousness is faith <u>on</u> Jesus, and Satan has already been fully judged <u>by</u> Jesus.

As we become fully persuaded of these truths and continue to grow from faith to faith in their reality, while remaining <u>patient</u>, then we will be ready to fully <u>manifest</u> as sons of God (Rom. 8:19). This is the "perfect work" of God in our lives. We are here to be translated from the man-created Kingdom of Lackitude to the Christ-created Kingdom of Plenitude. This is the voyage of the heart from death to life, wrath to love and darkness to light.

The Two Mountains

Plenitude and Lackitude are represented in Scriptures by the concepts of blessing and cursing. Plenitude is synonymous with blessing. Lackitude is synonymous with cursing. Deuteronomy 28 symbolically describes these two dynamics as mountains of decisions standing before us. Mount Gerizim was the mountain symbolizing blessing and Plenitude. Mount Ebal was the mountain symbolizing cursing and Lackitude. Let's consider these two dynamics.

Those in blessed Plenitude "hearken unto the voice of the Lord" (v.2). Those in cursed Lackitude "hearken not unto the voice of the Lord" (v.15). Those in blessed Plenitude are "overtaken in blessing" (v.2). Those in Lackitude are "overtaken in cursing" (v.15). Those in Plenitude are "blessed in the city and in the field" (v.3). Those in Lackitude are "cursed in the city and in the field" (v.16). Those in Plenitude are blessed in the "fruit" of their body and possessions (v.4). Those in Lackitude are cursed in the "fruit" of their body and possessions (v.18). Those in Plenitude are blessed in their eating and provision (v.5). Those in Lackitude are cursed in their eating and provision (v.17). Those in Plenitude are blessed whenever they come in and whenever they go out (v.6). Those in Lackitude are cursed whenever they go in and whenever they go out (v.19). Those in Plenitude have their spiritual enemies come against them one way but flee before them seven ways in complete rout (v.7). Those in Lackitude shall go out against their enemies one way but flee from them seven ways in complete rout (v.25). Those in Plenitude shall be blessed in their storehouses and in all the works of their hands (v.8). Those in Lackitude shall be cursed in their storehouses and in all the works of their hands (v.33-44). Those in blessed Plenitude shall be the head only and not the tail, above only and not beneath (v.13). Those in cursed Lackitude shall be the tail only and not the head, beneath only and not above (v.48-52).

Lackitude is a state of being which leaves us open and vulnerable to destructions of every kind. Neglecting the so great a salvation of God allows cursings to come and afflict us (Prov. 26:2). Plenitude is the absolute inoculation against cursing. However, these inoculations of God's goodness must be taken daily, or else our thoughts will dull, old thinking patterns return, and we will start to neglect our so great a salvation. Deuteronomy 28:47 instructs us on this very point when it tells us the cursings of Lackitude come, "Because thou servedst not the Lord thy God with joyfulness, and with gladness of heart, for the abundance of all things." In other words, when we lose patience (joyful endurance), which in this passage is described as "gladness of heart," we stop serving God in the Plenitude of blessing, which in this passage is described as "the abundance of all things."

Deuteronomy 28 goes even deeper into describing the cursing of Lackitude. Mental, emotional and physical sickness abound. In this depressed state of being, the Heavens above are as heavy as brass, the Earth below as hard as iron (v.23). The rain is as dust and powder (v.24), noonday is pitch dark and we are oppressed and spoiled evermore (v.29). We live in vexation and rebuke and whatever we set our hand to fails miserably (v.20). We suffer with madness, and blindness, and astonishment of heart (v.28). Our children will be taken prisoner by the ways of the world while we helplessly watch with longing to help them but having no might in our hands -- until we are literally driven mad by despair (v.32-34). We shall carry much seed into our fields, but shall gather little because the locust shall consume it (v.38). We will not be able to enjoy our spouses or houses because they will be taken away from us (v.30). In the morning we wish it was evening, and in the evening we wish it was morning (v.67). Our life "shall hang in doubt before" us and we "shalt fear day and night, and shalt have no assurance of life" (v.66). As stated previously, the bottom line of this cursed state is that we wish we were somewhere else with somebody else doing something else.

Which mountain do you desire for your life - - Mt. Gerizim and its blessings of Plenitude or Mt. Ebal and its cursings of Lackitude? If you desire Mt. Gerizim, then Mt. Ebal must be cast into the sea.

Entering the Promised Land of Plenitude

Let's take a fresh look at faith. It is always blessed to re-focus on the dynamic of faith. There is no pleasing God without it. **"But without faith it is impossible to please him:**

for he that cometh to God must believe that he is, and that he is a rewarder of them that diligently seek him.” Heb. 11:6. Moreover, only our faith can cast cursed Mt. Ebal into the sea. This is the mountain-moving faith spoken of in Mk. 11:23-24.

Let's take a closer look at this crucial faith passage. **“And Jesus answering saith unto them, Have faith in God. For verily I say unto you, That whosoever shall say unto this mountain, Be thou removed, and be thou cast into the sea; and shall not doubt in his heart, but shall believe that those things which he saith shall come to pass; he shall have whatsoever he saith. Therefore I say unto you, What things soever ye desire, when ye pray, believe that ye receive them, and ye shall have them.”** Mk. 11:22-24. Jesus instructs us at the outset of this passage to have the “faith <u>of</u> God” (see KJV margin note). Noted Greek scholars A. S. Warrell, A. T. Robertson and Ian Wallis all agree that Jesus in this passage is ordering us in the imperative mood to have the God-kind of faith - - i.e. the faith <u>of</u> God. What is the faith of God? How do we get it? How do we use it?

The faith of God is the faith of Jesus. Jesus <u>is</u> our righteousness (1 Cor. 1:30). “Righteousness” is defined in Scripture as the act of “believing God” (Rom. 4:3). If Jesus is <u>our</u> righteousness right now, then Jesus is <u>our</u> act of faith right now - - Jesus has sent <u>His</u> perfect faith to live and operate within us. Jesus commands us in Matthew 6:33 to seek <u>first</u> the Kingdom of God and <u>His</u> righteousness (i.e. the very faith <u>of</u> God revealed only in Christ Jesus). We are partakers of Jesus' divine nature (2 Pet. 1:3-5). We are not to live by our <u>own</u> faith but “by the faith <u>of</u> the Son of God” (Gal. 2:20). Hallelujah!

Now, notice how the faith of God is to work in Mark 11:23. First, faith "says." Faith is released through speech. Faith is certainly <u>possessed</u> by the heart, but faith is <u>released</u> into this earthly realm through the speech of man. Second, the speech that releases faith's power is spoken in the imperative mood - - speech that <u>orders</u> "mountainous" obstacles to be removed and cast into the sea. Third, the imperative speech that releases faith's power must flow from a heart of "certitude" which "doubts not." Remember that word "certitude?" It means "freedom from doubt." If these three dynamics are present - - speech, imperative mood and certitude - - then we shall have "whatsoever" we "saith."

Jesus helps us to further understand the concept of prayer, faith and Plenitude in Mark 11:24. Notice very carefully the wording used. Jesus says that "whatsoever things" we "desire" when "we pray," we are to "believe" that we "receive them" and we "shall have them." Notice that Jesus did <u>not</u> say that we need to believe that what we desire <u>will</u> <u>be</u> <u>given</u> to us by God. Rather, we are to believe we RECEIVE whatsoever things we desire. Do you see? Faith is not about believing God <u>will</u> give. Faith is about believing we are receiving now what God has <u>already</u> given us. This is Plenitude. THIS IS PLENITUDE!

If we read this passage with our natural understanding, we will miss it altogether. Faith doesn't <u>cause</u> God to <u>give</u>. Faith <u>enables</u> us to <u>receive</u>. Faith is hearing what God has always already freely given us and then giving it our "yes" and "amen," which then allows the manifestation of it to be released in <u>this</u> realm. This is why Paul calls <u>this</u> process "the hearing of faith."

Plenitude

The gift of the Holy Spirit is <u>received</u> by the "hearing of faith" (Gal. 3:2). All ministry of the Holy Spirit is done through "the hearing of faith" (Gal. 3:5). All miracles are worked by the "hearing of faith" (Gal. 3:5). "Faith cometh by hearing, and hearing by the Word of God." Rom. 10:17. In other words, <u>hearing</u> the "always already" promises from the Word of God ministered to us by the Holy Spirit. **"Now we have received, not the spirit of the world, but the spirit which is of God; that we might know the things that are freely given to us of God."** 1 Cor. 2:12. For those "called" of God, "hearing" that call through the Holy Spirit's promptings means everything. Many are called, but few hear. Many are saved, healed and delivered, but few have ever heard it called to them. To neglect God's so great a salvation is simply not to listen and hear the Holy Spirit calling us to fully believe what God has already done for us. God's calling requires faith's hearing. GOD'S CALLING REQUIRES FAITH'S HEARING. What is it that faith hears? The voice of God!

The Holy Ghost is the "voice" of God. To truly perform the Word of God is to perform His voice as we hear it call us into action. This voice lives in you as a born-again believer. This voice carries the character, authority and power of God. You can only incarnate the nature of Christ <u>if</u> and <u>as</u> you hearken to this voice. Only this voice accurately portrays the purposes and passions of God. Jesus always gave a pitch-perfect performance which reflected the exact image of His Heavenly Father, the very "image of the invisible God" (Col. 1:15). Because Jesus <u>always</u> heard His Father's voice, He always performed His Father's nature (Jn. 5:19,30).

Beloved, the voice is the key to everything. **"And it shall**

come to pass, if thou shalt hearken diligently unto the voice of the LORD thy God, to observe and to do all his commandments which I command thee this day, that the LORD thy God will set thee on high above all nations of the earth: And all these blessings shall come on thee, and overtake thee, if thou shalt hearken unto the voice of the LORD thy God. And the LORD shall make thee the head, and not the tail; and thou shalt be above only, and thou shalt not be beneath; if that thou hearken unto the commandments of the LORD thy God, which I command thee this day, to observe and to do them." Dt. 28:1-2,13. The first Adam rejected the voice of God (Gen. 3:8). The second Adam, Jesus, cleaved to the voice His whole life. Jesus has implanted into us, through the Baptism of the Holy Spirit, His own "cleaving strength" to hear the voice of God continually - - in all times and in all places. This is the mind of Christ - - to lock and load our focus on the voice of God.

Do you see? The Holy Spirit reveals to us the Plenitude of the finished work of Christ. Plenitude is not Plenitude if anything is left undone or incomplete. The Holy Spirit's ministry is to "voice" the completed and present reality of the Kingdom of Heaven.

Our problem is that rather than wholeheartedly believing the promises of God, we choose, by willpower or neglect, to walk by sight. We stop "listening" for the voice of the Holy Spirit and instead start walking by our own opinion about how things "look" to our natural mind. Walking by sight is the opposite of walking by faith. **"For we walk by faith, not by sight."** 2 Cor. 5:7. "Walking by sight" is known by different descriptions - - "judging by appearance," "leaning on our own understanding" and "idolatry."

Idolatry? How is walking by sight idolatrous? The Greek word for "idolatry" is "eidololatreia," and literally means "to worship or serve that which is seen." When 2 Corinthians 5:7 warns us not to walk by "sight," the word is "eidos" from which the Greek word for idolatry derives. Idolatry was the most common and serious sin in the Old Testament. In fact, the first two of the Ten Commandments prohibit the practice of idolatry. Every King of Israel or Judah was judged by how he dealt with the idolatry of his day. Some embraced idolatry like Jeroboam (1 Ki. 12:25-33). Others negligently allowed idolatry like Solomon (1 Ki. 11:1-13). Others tore down foreign idols but allowed false idols to Jehovah to remain like Jehoshaphat (2 Chr. 20:31-33). Finally, some great Kings like Josiah and Hezekiah destroyed all idolatry (2 Ki. 23:1-28; 2 Ki. 18:1-6).

Destroying idolatry is just as important today as it was back in the Old Testament. In fact, it's more important today because the body of Christ has the resources of a perfect King who stands ready, willing and able to tear down each and every idol in our lives. New Testament believers are told to flee idolatry (1 Cor. 10:14) because no idolater can inherit the Kingdom of God (Eph. 5:5). Jesus is the King of Kings, but we too are Kings in His service who will be judged on how hard we fight to tear down the high places of idolatry in our lives (Rev. 1:5-6).

The major difference between Old Testament idolatry and New Testament idolatry is that the Old focuses on external acts of idolatry while the New focuses on internal attitudes of idolatry. Our true battle is not against external idols but against internal mindsets. **"For though we walk in the flesh, we do not war after the flesh: (For the weapons of**

our warfare are not carnal, but mighty through God to the pulling down of strong holds;) Casting down imaginations, and every high thing that exalteth itself against the knowledge of God, and bringing into captivity every thought to the obedience of Christ; and having in a readiness to revenge all disobedience, when your obedience is fulfilled. Do ye look on things after the outward appearance?" 2 Cor. 10:3-7.

The last question in the above passage is my challenge to you. "Do ye look on things after the outward appearance?" If you do, then you are committing idolatry. Jesus said, **"Judge not according to the appearance, but judge righteous judgment."** Jn. 7:24. "Righteous judgment" means that we <u>never</u> bow to appalling appearances, crippling circumstances, discouraging details, oppressive opinions or hopeless hearts. Rather, we penetrate through, over and beyond all appearances to see the Lord's saving purpose, powerful provision and eager posture toward every situation of need.

This is the single-eye spoken of in Matthew 6:22, the focus that fills our whole body with light, the focus that sees Christ in all, through all and for all - - no matter how the situation may or may not "seem" or "appear." This leads us to another key to faith - - calling "those things that be not as though they were" (Rom. 4:17). Be careful. Very careful. This verse does not tell us that we are to call into being things that don't exist <u>anywhere</u>. Rather, we are to call things that "be not" <u>seen</u> in this realm as though they already "were," which they <u>are</u> in Heaven. We are to call things "here" on Earth as we "hear" by faith that they <u>already</u> exist in Heaven.

When you grasp this great truth, Plenitude will start to visibly manifest more and more as you verbally call forth what you spiritually see. Your first focus is not on what is visibly seen, but on what is visibly unseen.

The power of Plenitude lies in the <u>unseen</u> and it is here that your faith must learn to focus. To look at what is unseen seems impossible, but this is exactly what Scripture teaches us to do. **"We having the same spirit of faith, according as it is written, I believed, and therefore have I spoken; we also believe, and therefore speak. . . .While we look not at the things which are seen, but at the things which are not seen: for the things which are seen are temporal; but the things which are not seen are eternal."** 2 Cor. 4:13,18. Beloved, consider this important passage. It tells us that the "spirit of faith" believes and speaks <u>while</u> it looks at the things which are "not seen." The things not seen are the "eternal" purposes and promises of God already completed in Heaven. The unseen has far more power than the seen. In fact, "the things which are seen were not made of things which are visible" (Heb. 11:3). Moreover, "faith is the . . . evidence of things not seen" (Heb. 11:1), which is another way of saying our faith proves the power of the unseen. In other words, the miraculous fruit our faith produces <u>proves</u> that the power of the unseen can trump this visible world at any time and in any place.

Interlinear translations of Matthew 16:19 and 18:18 establish that Jesus literally tells Peter in the original Greek, "Whatever you bind or loose on Earth shall occur, having <u>already</u> been bound or loosed in Heaven." Heaven is the eternal <u>unseen</u> realm of Plenitude where all the "binding" of evil and the "loosing" of good has already occurred. We must learn to live in continual focus on these unseen realities. As we recognize and realize these realities through "the hearing of faith" promptings of the Holy Spirit, then we will verbally and imperatively bind and loose <u>here</u> what has already been bound and loosed in Heaven. What is already manifest in Heaven will now manifest here - - and now!

So what is it that we will bind? Lackitude. And what is it we will loose? Plenitude. Mount Ebal and its cursings are bound. Mount Gerizim and its blessings are loosed. Remember God has <u>already</u> "blessed us with all spiritual blessings in Heavenly places in Christ" (Eph. 1:3). God has <u>already</u> "raised us up together, and made us sit together in Heavenly places in Christ Jesus" (Eph. 2:6). All that comes from knowing God must be loosed and all that rises up against the knowledge of God must be bound. Bound and loosed <u>here</u> on Earth as it <u>already</u> is bound and loosed in Heaven.

We are surrounded by all the resources of Heaven. We have the anointing to access <u>all</u> these resources by the hearing of faith. We <u>know</u> all things (1 Jn. 2:20,27). We <u>possess</u> all things (1 Cor. 3:21). And we can <u>do</u> all things (Phil. 4:13). Remember, Lackitude is the mindset which will deny or doubt that you can know all things, possess all things and do all things. Plenitude is the mindset which will declare and convince you that the word of Plenitude is near you always, in your mouth and in your heart.

Practical Tips to Stay in Plenitude

1. <u>Confess the following Scriptural truths on a daily basis to keep Plenitude on the surface of your thoughts</u>:

   a. **"I rejoice evermore, pray without ceasing**

and in everything I give thanks, for this is the will of God in Christ Jesus for me." 1 Thes. 5:16-18.

b. "The love of God is shed abroad in my heart, by the Holy Spirit, supernatural love which thinks no evil, bears all things, believes all things, hopes all things, endures all things and never fails." Rom. 5:5; 1 Cor. 13:5-8.

c. "Whatsoever things are true, whatsoever things are honest, whatsoever things are just, whatsoever things are pure, whatsoever things are lovely, whatsoever things are of good report; if there be any virtue, and if there be any praise, I will continually think on these things." Phil. 4:8.

2. Develop a "Don't go there" mentality with yourself when thoughts of lack approach. Fear not. Worry not. Take no thought for the cares of the world. Seek first the Kingdom of God and His righteousness and all your needs will be added to you. Take captive any stray thought to the obedience of Christ. If rebellious thoughts attack, capture them and execute them with the truth of God. Take full vengeance on thoughts of lack. "For though we walk in the flesh, we do not war after the flesh: (For the weapons of our warfare are not carnal, but mighty through God to the pulling down of strong holds;) Casting down imaginations, and every high thing that exalteth itself against the knowledge of God, and bringing

into captivity every thought to the obedience of Christ; and having in a readiness to revenge all disobedience, when your obedience is fulfilled." 2 Cor. 10:3-6.

3. Repent "quickly" if you do fall into Lackitude. Repentance is a way <u>out</u> of Lackitude, not a way <u>into</u> it. Many continue to endlessly beat themselves for wrong mindsets, when in truth self-condemnation itself is a wrong mindset. Many wrongly think self-condemnation <u>is</u> repentance. Wrong. Repentance is changing the way you think - - right now. Don't think you have to serve a long prison sentence of self-loathing and self-flagellation. The moment you repent, God is able to immediately work positive energy and affirming power within you. **"Now I rejoice, not that ye were made sorry, but that ye sorrowed to repentance: for ye were made sorry after a godly manner, that ye might receive damage by us in nothing. For godly sorrow worketh repentance to salvation not to be repented of: but the sorrow of the world worketh death. For behold this selfsame thing, that ye sorrowed after a godly sort, what carefulness it wrought in you, yea, what clearing of yourselves, yea, what indignation, yea, what fear, yea, what vehement desire, yea, what zeal, yea, what revenge! In all things ye have approved yourselves to be clear in this matter."** 2 Cor. 7:9-11.

4. Think the best toward all creation. Only the best. Always the best. Have continual goodwill toward all. Avoid all accusations toward other men. Forgive all

men their trespasses at all times (Lk. 11:4). Judge not other men, but if you are called to judge the "spirit" of a situation, judge the righteous judgment. Remember, our enemies are not <u>men</u> but false ideas which rise up in our lives against the knowledge of God. Make sure your first thought toward any situation is your best thought. Our first best thought will always be toward "the hearing of faith" which reveals the Lord's love toward all situations - - supernatural love which bears all things, believes all things, hopes all things, endures all things and never fails.

5. <u>Stay focused on the unseen and eternal</u> (2 Cor. 4:18; Heb. 11:3). When Jesus ascended from this seen realm into the unseen realm of Heaven, His <u>being</u> became our Plenitude. In Christ "we live and move and have our being" (Acts 17:28). The "in Christ" realities of the New Testament describe our new "environment" in which the blessings of God are always beside us, inside us, over us and beneath us. Jesus has been made <u>unto</u> us wisdom and righteousness and sanctification and redemption (1 Cor. 1:30). We are able to "put on the Lord Jesus" because His favor is always within arm's reach (Rom. 13:14). All we must do is learn to continually believe and receive the "cloaking of Christ" over our entire being and in all our ways. The Lord Jesus Christ has become the great unseen! Plenitude's source is the unseen Kingdom of God which surrounds us and permeates us. As we learn to serve the Lord "with gladness of heart, for the abundance of all things" (Dt. 28:47), <u>then</u> shall the blessings of Plenitude overtake us and manifest the glory of God into this earthly realm.

Purpose in your heart that you will not walk by sight, appearance, circumstance and natural understanding. You will not worship what is seen with your fear, dread, worry, lust or pride. Actual lack, fear of lack or threat of lack will not steal your single-eye. Rather, your laser-like focus will be on Plenitude's power of abundance.

6. Imagine Plenitude as both invisible sockets of spiritual power and invisible pockets of spiritual provision which are always located at either side of you, on your right hand and on your left. Imagine that you at anytime can stick both your hands into these sockets to release the power of Plenitude into the "now" (2 Cor. 6:7). Your hands are anointed with the Plenitude of God. You "shall lay hands on the sick and they shall recover" (Mk. 16:18). Only empty hands can plug into these sockets. The vain works of our hands must be emptied of pride, ambition, strife, competitiveness and jealousy. When our hearts are full of faith and our hands empty of vanity, then we will plug into Plenitude's power. "Wholehearted empty-handedness" is what I like to call this dynamic. Scriptures call this quality "importunity" in Luke 11:5-8. Here, the man had "nothing" in his hands but "everything" in his heart to know his friend would open the door of provision to him. Jesus commended and commanded this same quality for us. **"And I say unto you, Ask, and it shall be given you; seek, and ye shall find; knock, and it shall be opened unto you. For every one that asketh receiveth; and he that seeketh findeth; and to him that knocketh it shall be opened."** Lk. 11:9-10. What opens the door

of Plenitude is our wholehearted empty-handedness. My children, when they were young, would often stick their hands in my pockets seeking to pull out a blessing - - candy, coins, etc. They knew dad's pockets were full. So should we stick our hands into our Abba-Father's pockets of Plenitude and pull out pre-ordained blessings in our time of need. What great imagery! Pockets and sockets. Pockets of Plenitude's provision and sockets of Plenitude's power. What a mighty God we serve! Jesus reached His hands into His Abba's pockets to produce mass amounts of bread, fish, healings, exorcisms and miracles. And so can we!

7. <u>Always distinguish Plenitude from optimism</u>. Plenitude is God-made while optimism is man-made. Optimism merely sees the glass half-full, while Plenitude sees the glass running over. "My cup runneth over." Ps. 23:5. Optimism looks to the future to make things better, while Plenitude looks to the accomplished past that things are <u>already</u> made better. Optimism is not faith. Optimism often disguises itself as faith. Optimism still walks by sight. It just tries to re-interpret what "is" in a more positive way. For instance, pessimism says the glass is half-empty while optimism says the glass is half-full. However, we are still only dealing with a glass with a water volume of 50%. It is the exact <u>same</u> "appearance" under either view. There are just two different ways of describing the same thing. What appears remains exactly the same. An optimist may say, "I believe God can, might or even will heal you." A pessimist may say, "I don't believe God will, might or even can heal you." But both are

merely describing the same appearance in a different way. Sickness still "is" and only <u>future</u> action by God can be debated. Instead, Plenitude says, "Rise up and be healed now as you have already been healed in Heaven by the Cross of Christ." Here, Plenitude focuses on past action of God which is now beyond debate or opinion. Seen from this angle, optimism is merely the "good" on the *Tree of the Knowledge of Good and Evil*, while pessimism is the "evil." Both produce death. Both are from Lackitude. Pessimism is undisguised Lackitude. Optimism is disguised Lackitude. I have seen so many "optimistically" try to apply their faith and fail. I myself have fallen into this type of failure many times. The reason it fails is because it is focused on what God *can\will\might* do in the future rather than on what God has *always\ already\fully* done in the past. If you find yourself debating what God may or may not do, you are starting off in an unblessed place. You may optimistically think God "will" do a certain thing. But this way of thinking requires you to believe God hasn't always already done everything there is to do about all <u>present</u> and <u>future</u> situations through the <u>past</u> completed work of Christ. Remember, in God's foreknowledge and unsurpassable power He has always already prepared and predestinated us to a life full of good works which exist <u>only</u> in the completed "rest" of God which now awaits us. We can only "work" righteously when we learn to "rest" completely. What is it we are resting in? The finished work of God toward us, for us and within us. What a beautiful truth to relax and abide within. Relaxing in this truth releases the resources of Heaven like a flood. As the Church, we are gatekeepers of this blessed flood. Listen and rejoice in Paul's prayer of Plenitude toward the Ephesians which gloriously reveals the Church <u>already</u> triumphant. **"Wherefore I also, after I heard of your faith in the Lord Jesus, and love unto all the saints, Cease not to give thanks for you, making mention of you in my prayers; That the God of our Lord Jesus Christ, the Father of glory, may give unto you the spirit of wisdom and revelation in the knowledge of him: The eyes of your understanding being enlightened; that ye may know what is the hope of his calling, and what the riches of the glory of his inheritance in the saints, and what is the exceeding greatness of his power to us-ward who believe, according to the working of his mighty power, Which he wrought in Christ, when he raised him from the dead, and set him at his own right hand in the heavenly places, Far above all principality, and power, and might, and dominion, and every name that is named, not only in this world, but also in that which is to come: and hath put all things under his feet, and gave him to be the head over all things to the church, Which is his body, the fullness of him that filleth all in all."** Eph. 1:15-23.

8. <u>Make Plenitude your "big idea."</u> Invest all that you think, believe and feel into this notion. It is true. It's got to be true. Scriptures demand it. Faith demands it. God demands it. The world is flooded with ideas. Ideas grow into ideologies. Ideologies grow into strongholds. The "biggest idea" in your life wins. It will control what you think, how you think and

the way you emotionally process reality. I have seen people die prematurely because the "idea" of death consumed all their thoughts and emotions. When a doctor informed my mother decades ago that chemotherapy had not helped her cancer, she was dead in two weeks, despite the fact that doctors were giving her six months to a year to live. The idea of death became her "big idea." At that time I didn't have the faith to share a bigger idea with her. She lost her mind within a week of the bad report. Then her body shut down and she was gone. Am I saying she didn't have cancer? No, of course not. I <u>am</u> saying that nobody in our family had the idea of Plenitude we could draw on for strength. Ideas can create reality. The idea of liberty produced this nation, civil rights and the Constitution. Satan's idea of disobedience produced sickness, oppression, disasters, wars, cursings, sin and death. The greater idea of Plenitude will swallow <u>all</u> lesser ideas of sin and death <u>as</u> you let it. And you let it by Plenitude becoming your pearl of great value. You sell <u>every</u> other idea you have about what *should\could\might* happen and trade it all for this glorious truth of Plenitude which is too good not to be true - - we have already been delivered from all evil by the precious blood of Christ. Make this your "big idea."

9. <u>Plenitude brings us imperative faith.</u> "Therefore thus says the Lord . . . If you take out the precious from the vile, you shall be as My mouth." Jer. 15:19. Plenitude is the mind of Christ which extracts the precious from the vile. Plenitude rescues the Godly remnant in any situation or circumstance. Plenitude is the re-

port of the Lord which heroically highlights God's active and available goodness through all trial and tribulation. The Jeremiah verse above assures us that when we are able to penetrate <u>all</u> appearances with the plenitude of God, <u>then</u> we will be as His mouth. In other words, we will speak in the imperative just as God speaks in the imperative <u>when</u> we learn to take out the precious from the vile in each and every situation we encounter. All too often we focus on and emphasize the "vile" we encounter, rather than declaring the salvation of God which is an ever present help in time of need. The point is that we will never manifest the imperative faith of *The Jesus Mood* until we learn to abide in Plenitude. Plenitude automatically activates imperative faith which automatically manifests *The Jesus Mood* in all its glory.

10. <u>You are predestined for Plenitude.</u> "Ye have not chosen me, but I have chosen you, and ordained you, that ye should go and bring forth fruit, and that your fruit should remain: that whatsoever ye shall ask of the Father in my name, he may give it you." Jn. 15:16. Remember from Chapter One that "ask" in the above passage is translated from a Greek word which means, "strictly a demand of something due." To ask this way is to both "demand" and "command" a result in the imperative mood. However, the key part of this passage reveals that we are "chosen" and "ordained" to bear the "fruit" which is to "remain." What is this fruit? Imperative faith! We are ordained and predestined so that "whatsoever" we demand and command in the name (the very nature and very mood) of Jesus will be given to us

by the Father. In other words, God has commanded us to command. We don't issue imperatives of faith because we choose to, but we issue imperatives of faith because we are predestined to "bring forth" this fruit. This is great news! You can't produce imperative faith. You can only obey it. It is not a question of ability. It is a question of obedience. The "determinate counsel and foreknowledge of God" has already implanted, imbedded and imparted *The Jesus Mood* deep into your spirit. Seize your destiny by the hilt and pull your sword of imperative authority out of the rock of ages Who indwells you. Wield this sword of imperative faith over every trial and tribulation you face. Command and demand the works of God to manifest in all your spheres of influence. Always remember, God commands you to command. Like the Roman Centurion, your authority to give commands comes solely from your willingness to obey commands.

11. Read the following poem on a regular basis and meditate on its truths.

PLENITUDE

Each dawn I lie awake,
Two roads before me I may take.

The first road is called Lackitude,
Dark is its path and dismal its mood.

Traveling on it all things I do track,
Through my own bitter eyes of judgment and lack.

All things fall short on this low road of shame,
Every aspect of life is infected with blame.

The cracks on creation never seem to be sealed,
The cracks are projected from our eyes left unhealed.

A prisoner's despair defines our start,
From here the battle for joy loses heart.

No shortcoming escapes our detection,
Children, wives, husbands all fail our inspection.

Disappointed moms, disapproving dads,
Disheartened daughters and disillusioned lads.

Like a killing cancer Lackitude does spread,
Into all our souls' corners it poisons with dread.

We no longer see events aright or in light,
And our darkened response is to fight or to flight.

This fever of flawed seeing,
Corrupts our whole being.

This road of Lackitude is the road of sure death,
So gird up your loins and take a deep breath.

The second road is the path we must measure,
All its road signs reflect God's limitless treasure.

Plenitude is the name of this way most divine,
The journey is pure joy and the view so sublime.

Instead of a mindset which causes us to sour,
Plenitude focuses on fulness and power.

The more we travel the road of Plenitude,
Our eyesight improves as well as our mood.

We no longer look at things as they seem,
Instead we behold with God's eye of true gleam.

The Lord Jesus Christ had God's sight 20\20,
Seeing Abba's provisions through the eyes of pure plenty.

His mind never wandered, diverted or doubted,
His hope never squandered, perverted or routed.

The appearance of things Jesus judged not,
The surface of things to Him was mere rot.

Instead, Jesus saw the evidence of things not seen,
His Father's will to all goodness He did continually glean.

What Christ saw in each and every man,
Was His Father's image and ultimate plan.

Lost and scattered sheep were all that He saw,
As God's good shepherd, Christ did rescue them all.

Jesus the shepherd gave His life for the fold,
The Cross that He bore was the rescue foretold.

Three days in the grave caused many to doubt,
But the power of love brought the ultimate rout.

Death and deception no longer ran free,
Christ has created a greater reality.

After He ascended the best news arrived,
At Pentecost's coming Christ <u>in</u> us now did reside.

No longer must men walk the Lackitude road,
Heavy laden with oppression and burdensome load.

The sunny side has become a street,
To this place of joy we must direct our feet.

Plenitude sees God's provisions as "always already,"
This central resolve keeps us strong and ever steady.

Whereas Lackitude moans "never good enough,"
Plenitude pulls diamonds from the rough.

Adam and Eve in Plenitude did reign,
Till the serpent did bite them with Lackitude's fang.

Before the bite, "un"self-aware in their bliss,
They did walk in God's garden and experience His kiss.

In naked submission they knew not their own will,
But then came the serpent with a most bitter pill.

The lie came from Satan that something was wrong,
God was hiding something to them which belonged.

The serpent beguiled with his continual hissing,
Every lie that came forth described what was missing.

Did God truly say? Don't you want to be wise?
Take of this fruit and open your eyes.

Then you will know what it's like to be God,
Instead of mere humans, clueless and odd.

The couple did eat the forbidden fruit of desire,
Their hearts were now hardened by the father of liars.

The couple now feared the God who gave them life,
Where once they had full blessing, they now only had strife.

Afraid, ashamed and now self-aware,
They hid behind fig leaves of pride and despair.

Their only defense to their first degree sin,
Was to point the finger elsewhere again and again.

The man blamed the woman whom God did provide,
While the woman blamed the snake with Satan inside.

Neither human stepped up to the plate,
To repent of their evil and admit their mistake.

This then is how the curse began,
Its poison now spread in every woman and man.

Then and now, an accusation of God's lack,
Does start each and every spiritual attack.

If you would prepare well for Lackitude's defeat,
Then let your mind only the noble, virtuous and praisewor-
thy keep.

Mark it well, my beloved, the option is yours,
Two roads confront you and both have their doors.

If you set your mind on the Lackitude road,
Its door will slam shut on you while its curses unfold.

But if you set your mind on Plenitude's street,
Its door will fly open and freedom you'll greet.

So trust not your thoughts 'til you establish their source,
Don't taste any flavor unless it's on Plenitude's course.

Every new word we chew with our minds,
Leads to the next thought and either looses or binds.

The "now" determines the next,
So "Plenitude Now!" must be your text.

Toward Lackitude be in constant denial,
Let not one word, thought or emotion put you on trial.

For the words which we speak reveal our true heart,
And our true heart is where both roads get their start.

Out of our heart-abundance our mouth always speaks,
As the words we release reveal one of the two streets.

Use words of life if you want to live,
Evict words of death and be quick to forgive.

We must learn to believe only the Lord's good reports,
For Plenitude always trumps what Lackitude distorts.

All will be well, all will be well,
Christ has "always already" defeated death and all Hell.

Chapter 5
Performing the Word

The Jesus Mood comes down to this: we are called to be "doers of the Word" (Jas. 1:22). The Word of God must be "performed" upon the Earth. The history of the early Church was called the Book of Acts. Acts are completed ac-tions performed by actors. We are called to not just "hear" our calling but also to perform it. The word "perform" means to "carry out or execute an action or process." The Scriptures are promises of God we "perform" into being. To perform a Scripture is to believe it, belove it and bespeak it.

The King James Version does not just say to believe in Christ, but to believe on Christ. Believing just in Him is merely "in-formative," but believing on Him is "performative." To pray in the imperative mood of Jesus is to perform God's Word unto manifestation in this earthly realm. I know that when I pray in the imperative, I feel the words come up burning from my belly through my heart and out of my mouth. This is the Holy Spirit enriching and empowering my words to speak salvation into situations - - salvation which reconciles reality to the will of God.

Jesus gave us keys to the Kingdom of God - - the binding and loosing authority to command Heaven's will to appear on Earth (Matt. 16:19; 18:18). Jesus displayed this exact same authority during His ministry. He "performed" the works of His Father, not His <u>own</u> works but the works of His Father. Don't miss this. **"But Jesus answered them, My Father worketh hitherto, and I work . . . .Then answered Jesus and said unto them, Verily, verily, I say unto you, The Son can do nothing of himself, but what he seeth the Father do: for what things soever he doeth, these also doeth the Son likewise."** Jn. 5:17,19. Jesus lived in a continual state of hearing and allowing the Father's works to be <u>performed</u> through Him. Jesus lovingly permitted His Heavenly Father's presence to fully inhabit Him. **"Believest thou not that I am in the Father, and the Father in me? the words that I speak unto you I speak not of myself: but the Father that dwelleth in me, he doeth the works. Believe me that I am in the Father, and the Father in me: or else believe me for the very works' sake. Verily, verily, I say unto you, He that believeth on me, the works that I do shall he do also; and greater works than these shall he do; because I go unto my Father. And whatsoever ye shall ask in my name, that will I do, that the Father may be glorified in the Son. If ye shall ask any thing in my name, I will do it."** Jn. 14:10-14.

The enormity of the above passage cannot be overstated. Just as Jesus performed the works of His Father by allowing His Father full habitation, we can perform the works of Jesus by allowing Jesus full habitation within us. **"If ye abide in me, and my words abide in you, ye shall ask what ye will, and it shall be done unto you."** Jn. 15:7. Don't we all know "deep down" that we are "called" to "perform" the "wonderful works of God?" The disciples certainly knew this. **"Then said they unto him, What shall we do, that we might work the works of God? Jesus answered and said unto them, This is the work of God, that ye believe on him whom he hath sent."** Jn. 6:28-29. Remember, to believe "on" Jesus requires an affirmative "act" of our yielding to His habitation.

Acting teachers will tell you there are only two kinds of actors - - those who inhabit their roles and those who allow the role to inhabit them. The first type are mere pretenders. The second type are true artists who allow something greater to literally possess them. In other words, poor actors give fake performances while remaining ever the same. Great actors give true performances while always becoming something different and greater.

Acting is a much maligned profession. It is often full of vain and self-centered people who live for the praise of men and not God. However, as an art form, it is unique. It is the only profession which, at its best, focuses on discerning, discovering and developing authentic inner-motivations for all our actions. The good actor always asks, "What's my motivation?" Very few people <u>ever</u> ask this most important question. Christianity is likewise focused on this same question of motive. **"For the word of God is quick, and powerful, and sharper than any twoedged sword, piercing even to the dividing asunder of soul and spirit, and of the joints and marrow, and is a discerner of the thoughts and in-**

tents of the heart." Heb. 4:12.

The application for Christians is obvious. For me to be a *doer\actor\performer* of the Word of God, I will either "fake it" by doing works under my own efforts <u>or</u> I will truly perform God's Word by allowing the Spirit of Christ to fully anoint my motives and actions with His power and presence. In other words, I can wrongly try to inhabit the role of a Christian with my <u>own</u> righteousness. Or, I can rightly allow the Spirit of Christ to inhabit me with <u>His</u> righteousness. This difference makes all the difference. Let's get some practical pointers from the greatest acting teacher of all time. Acting at its worst is a profession of pure pretend and fakery. But, at its best it seeks purity of being, truth within and beauty without.

The Method

At the outset, I must confess two things. First, once upon a time I was a stage actor. I acted in numerous plays in high school and college. I was even a drama major at college for two years and took several acting classes. Second, I was not a very good actor. I had no sense of true performance. I just tried to imitate certain movie stars I admired. I was very loud and forceful, but I lacked any substance, depth or emotional content. I eventually switched majors.

I remember in my acting classes studying the works of an acting teacher named Konstantin Stanislavski (1865-1938). I didn't pay close attention then, but I do now. He is considered the greatest acting teacher of all time. He taught acting at the Moscow Art Theater and is revered as the founder of "the Method" - - a system of acting which seeks to produce inspired, authentic and meaningful performances.

Before we get into "the Method," let's first look at what the art of acting was like in Stanislavski's day. Actually, it wasn't even "art" in Stanislavski's eyes. He was disturbed at all the fakery, exaggeration and unrealistic posturing actors were using. Stanislavski saw these actors as "clowns" rather than "artists," clowns who were corrupting great plays with "plastic" performances. Actors back then would never speak in their natural voices but spoke their lines in a completely artificial manner. Each word was accompanied by some grand and exaggerated gesture of the body. Whenever an actor finished a long monologue and began to exit the stage, he would raise his right arm and keep it raised until he was gone from the sight of the audience. Our modern-day response to such theatrical corniness would be one of eye-rolling disgust. Stanislavski agreed.

Before Stanislavski, drama schools only taught external elements of acting through ballet, fencing, voice, speech and diction. There was no inner acting technique. Actors learned to memorize mechanical movements, artificial poses and ornate speaking. Stanislavski himself learned all these external techniques studying posture and facial expressions in a mirror. He learned mechanical ways of memorizing and reciting lines. He studied ballet and opera. For years he taught the key to good acting lay in externals: costumes, makeup, props, facial expressions, voice styles, walking styles, etc. However, Stanislavski continued to feel "false" on stage and that he was "engaged in evil work."

Stanislavski became convinced that the missing element was "truth." The primary calling of an actor was to discover the truth of the inner life of the character and then to express this dynamic to the audience in an authentic and inspired performance. Actors create ever-new human beings, each with a unique inner world and vibrant human spirit. This is what it is all about for Stanislavski - - "the life of the human spirit." The goal of art had to be the "spiritual communication" of truth between, among and for people. Between the audience and actors. Among the actors on stage. And for the benefit of all mankind.

Stanislavski believed in <u>incarnation</u>, which essentially means "spirit taking on flesh." The actor's calling was to embody the spirit of the character to make it clear to the audience in every way. Stanislavski demanded from his students that all performances contain profound truth, simplicity and naturalness. His motto was, "Go <u>from</u> yourself," then go <u>to</u> the character and create the inner experiences, incarnate them and then perform them in an understandable way to the audience. Profound spiritual experience for both audience and cast was the goal of all acting performances.

Stanislavski started a revolution, but he didn't finish it. To this day, there is still a debate within acting schools as to which is the preferred style of performance - - pretending or incarnating. In other words, should the actor inhabit the role or should the role inhabit the actor? British acting schools largely train actors to inhabit the role with external techniques, while American acting schools largely train actors to allow the role to inhabit them by use of internal techniques.

Stanislavski's internal techniques have been corporately labeled "the Method." The term Method-acting refers to Stanislavski's approach. At its root, the Method rejects purely external theatrics in favor of a realistic style in which the actor seeks to identify, or "live," his role.

So, what can we learn from Stanislavski? As Christians, what can the art of acting teach us? Well, the parallels and applications are amazing and fun to consider. Acting provides the perfect parable of walking in the Spirit of Christ - - that is, the <u>very</u> nature and <u>very</u> character of Christ.

Are we called to inhabit Christ by imitating and pretending to be <u>like</u> Him, or are we called to allow Christ to actually and literally indwell us with His personality and presence? Are we to be Christians who pretend or Christians who incarnate? The answer is obvious. Jesus <u>is</u> God incarnate. Jesus now seeks to incarnate us through the inner working of the Holy Spirit. Jesus Himself works in us to <u>will</u> and to <u>do</u>, to <u>believe</u> and to <u>act</u>, to <u>love</u> and to <u>live</u>. This is our "role" of a lifetime.

But what about the audience? As Christians, do we have an audience watching our spiritual performances? Yes! The "cloud of witnesses" in Hebrews 12:1 suggests all the saints of old are watching and cheering us on. Angels are also watching us as those who "desire to look into" the things being revealed in us (1 Pet. 1:12). The world also watches our lives with a wondering eye (Acts 1:8). Satan obviously watches us with an accusing eye to condemn us (Rev. 12:10). Lastly, God is always observing all things at all times (Prov. 15:3). Yes, we all are continually before a huge audience, both seen and unseen.

Do you see? We are all actors in the production of the Kingdom of God. Just as the Bible describes "actions" of "righteous actors," we are called to likewise perform the works of God as actors of righteousness, doers of the Word who have "put on the Lord Jesus Christ" (Rom. 13:14). This is

The Jesus Mood. The imperative faith of Jesus incarnates us to perform as manifest sons of God (Rom. 8:19). Only this "Method" produces authentic performance. *The Jesus Mood* is the Jesus Method - - incarnation, incarnation, incarnation.

When I rehearsed in college plays, the director often chided me, "STAY IN CHARACTER!" This was because I continually joked around with the other actors. I obviously was not a Method actor. A method actor always stays in character. What a great exhortation for Christians, "STAY IN CHARACTER." In other words, abide and remain in the presence, character and nature of Jesus - - at all times. Don't break character at home, work, play or ministry. Be consistent. Be constant. When we break character we lose spiritual "rhythm," "tempo" and "momentum," terms Stanislavski used to describe the proper mood of the character. When an actor finds the right tempo and rhythm for his character, all movements become natural. Speech becomes profound and emotional content abounds. As one stays in this tempo and rhythm, momentum builds in every scene toward the climax of the play. Beloved, as Christians stay in the "rhythm of rest" and the "tempo of truth," something wonderful happens - - momentum builds for greater and greater anointing.

Our greatest enemies here are tension and self-awareness. Tension includes stress, fear, worry, dread, frustration and impatience. These toxic elements cause us to break character again and again. We feel defiled and it is difficult to get back into Christian character.

Stanislavski saw that proper focus removes barriers of tension. He received this revelation watching ocean waves crash against the hard and jagged rocks. Water and land were battling each other. Yet, up the beach, where there weren't any rocks, the tide smoothly interacted with the sand. When an actor concentrates the right way, it produces a relaxed state which removes rocks from the shoreline of our hearts, rocks of tension which cause us to battle ourselves within. The heart is now free to be washed over by waves of spiritual inspiration and motivation <u>without</u> the presence of tension. Doesn't Scripture describe "rocky heart soil" as that condition of the heart which is shallow and unrooted (Mk. 4:16-17)? In other words, this divided heart has so many rocks of tension barricading it against the ocean of the Spirit, that it simply can't keep its root in God. Tension can be a deadly enemy.

Similarly, self-awareness is another great impediment to staying in character. Stanislavski famously said, "Lose the mirror!" The mirror "teaches men to look at the outside rather than the inside of his soul." The act of looking in a mirror to test to see if we are in character actually breaks character because we become self-aware. For the Christian, this is dangerous. Adam and Eve fell from natural nakedness to tension-full self-awareness. They broke character. The book of James tells us that an unstable, double-minded man likes to look in a mirror and behold his natural face, but by so doing immediately forgets his true self. The Apostle Paul became so unaware of self that he made this amazing statement, "I judge not mine own self. For I know nothing by myself; but he that judgeth me is the Lord." 1 Cor. 4:3-4. Paul lost the mirror. And so can we. Stanislavski called this master key to true performance "Directed Attention."

Directed Attention

Stanislavski saw that our focus determines everything. A child's focus always is on what the child is interested in and only what the child is interested in. A child always focuses on what is seen or what appears before him. This is why children often fail to pay attention to instructions about matters unseen. However, adults are different. Adults can direct their attention to something they are not currently interested in or which does not yet presently appear to the "naked eye." In other words, we can direct our attention solely by our will-power. This is what Stanislavski called the "iron will" of the actor.

Thus, the iron will locked onto any subject will then produce interest in and enthusiasm for the subject. Do you see? For the immature, interest brings focus. But for the mature, focus brings interest. Fallen man does not perceive God because he is not interested in God. But as a willing man focuses more and more on the things of God, interest grows, passion grows, love grows and grows and grows. God is not hiding. We are.

Be careful. Our iron will can do nothing but focus. It can't be God. It can't create God. It can't accurately imitate God. It cannot work the righteousness of God. But what it can do is pay attention. It can yield its focus to God. It can allow incarnation by the power of the Holy Spirit. It can look and listen for the prompting of God. It can set its focus on the unseen but ever present Kingdom of God.

"Directed Attention" speaks of mental alertness, emotional availability and physical readiness. Consider these verses:

"Wherefore gird up the loins of your mind, be sober, and hope to the end for the grace that is to be brought unto you at the revelation of Jesus Christ." 1 Pet. 1:13.

"Delight thyself also in the LORD; and he shall give thee the desires of thine heart." Ps. 37:4.

"I beseech you therefore, brethren, by the mercies of God, that ye present your bodies a living sacrifice, holy, acceptable unto God, which is your reasonable service." Rom. 12:1.

Do you see? "Directed Attention" focuses our spirit, soul and body on the Kingdom of God. Focus <u>then</u> harvests light, peace and sanctification. **"And thou shalt love the Lord thy God with all thy heart, and with all thy soul, and with all thy mind, and with all thy strength: this is the first commandment."** Mk. 12:30. **"The light of the body is the eye: if therefore thine eye be single, thy whole body shall be full of light."** Matt. 6:22.

I want to share seven keys Stanislavski taught about "Directed Attention." As we apply these to our Christian walk, we will be able to better focus <u>on</u> and yield <u>to</u> the Holy Spirit.

Directed Attention Key #1 - *Receive the Script*

The Script for a Christian is the Bible. Scripture is the "Script" of who "u" really "re." Scripture is the Script of who you <u>really</u> are. You must believe this. You cannot direct your attention fully to the Bible until you receive it as <u>the</u> inspired Script for your life. *"God's Word is supernatural in origin, eternal in duration; inexpressible in valor; infinite in scope; regenerative in power; infallible in authority; universal in application; inspired in totality. Read it through; write it down; pray it in; work it out; pass it on. The Word of God changes a man until he becomes an Epistle of God."* Smith Wigglesworth.

However, our Script isn't just the Bible. The Lord has predestined us to walk in good works, blessed events and divine encounters (Eph. 1:5, 11; 2:10; Rom. 8:29). Our specific destiny is written in "the volume of the book" (Ps. 40:7; 139:16; Heb. 10:7). What is this "volume of the book?" Where is it? Who wrote it? Well, obviously, God wrote it. The book is located in Heaven. As to what it is, it is "the Lamb's Book of Life" (Rev. 21:27). Simply put, the Lord has a supernatural Script, a director's Script with margin notes filled with express plans and production notes for every scene of our lives. His Script and His direction to us through our "hearing of faith" will allow the Book of Life to "manifest" our predestiny in Plenitude. Remember, your Bible is your Script given you by your Divine Director - - the Lord Jesus Christ. But, God continues to retain the "Director's Script" which has all the specific plans and purposes for Christians, both individually and corporately. This Script can only be accessed by interaction with and instruction from the Holy Spirit.

Directed Attention Key #2 -
Meditate, Memorize and Mutter the Script

A good actor has to know his lines. He must first read the Script, then study the Script, then rehearse the Script. The Scriptures must become second nature to us. Then they will become our first nature. The Hebrew word for "meditate" in the following verse actually means to "murmur" or "utter." In other words, meditation is accomplished by speaking and rehearsing Scripture out loud. **"This book of the law shall not depart out of thy mouth; but thou shalt meditate (utter) therein day and night, that thou mayest observe to do according to all that is written therein: for then thou shalt make thy way prosperous, and then thou shalt have good success."** Jsh. 1:8. I have written a book on this most important topic entitled *Lift Up Your Jawbone*. It will bless you. Confessing Scripture out loud on a daily basis is a vital spiritual discipline. It is the very best way to internalize the Scriptures. The Word becomes flesh in us as we heart-receive it, mind-memorize it, and tongue-rehearse it. These are not three different things, but one focused thing. To recite Scripture is to meditate and receive it. To heartily receive the Word of God is to confess and meditate it. To meditate Scripture is to heartily receive and recite it. There is a Hebrew word which describes this single-eyed focus on Scripture. The word is "Kavanah." It means "wholehearted concentration" or "passionate intention." It is this quality which prevents our confessions from becoming vain repetitions. Kavanah is Directed Attention on the Lord's presence which inhabits, infuses and incarnates all the "exceeding great and precious promises" of Scripture. This process plants the promises of God into all our soul's soils, both conscious and unconscious. This is the first step of allowing incarnation - - internalizing the Scripture.

Directed Attention Key #3 - *Understand the Script's Subtext*

"Subtext" refers to the meaning of the Script behind and between the words. It is the meaning the author intended to be conveyed <u>not</u> through what the text literally says, but rather what the text spiritually means. Stanislavski taught that the subtext makes up 90% of the story, while the literal text makes up 10%. He compared it to an iceberg. The bulk of it is unseen underneath the water with only the tip in plain view. So too, the Bible's subtext can only be revealed by the illumination of the Holy Spirit. While the literal "by the letter" reading certainly can be helpful, how much more crucial is our need to spiritually read and absorb the subtext of Scripture. **"Not that we are sufficient of ourselves to think any thing as of ourselves; but our sufficiency is of God; Who also hath made us able ministers of the new testament; not of the letter, but of the spirit: for the letter killeth, but the spirit giveth life."** 2 Cor. 3:5-6. I remember when I acted on stage that I had no idea of how important the subtext of the Script was for an actor. I honestly didn't care. I just tried to speak my lines with force and style. I didn't know the heart of the author, or what he was trying to spiritually convey with my role in the play. I just read "the letter" of the Script. As the above passage says, the letter kills. And my "by the letter" performances certainly killed the audiences' interest and enjoyment. However, the Spirit gives life to those who direct their attention to the subtext of the Bible. This allows us as righteous doers of the Word to give inspired performances which will fulfill the Scriptures by revealing the inner thoughts, intents and motivations of the divine Author of our faith. The basic subtext of Scripture is always and only this, "God is good." **"This then is the message which we have heard of him, and declare unto you, that God is light, and in him is no darkness at all."** 1 Jn. 1:5. The world only sees the tip of this truth. The more we understand God's goodness beneath the surface of all things, we can then "perform" this goodness to manifest in plain view. The glacier of God's goodness will fully surface. **"And we know that all things work together for good to them that love God, to them who are the called according to his purpose."** Rom. 8:28.

Directed Attention Key #4 -
Understand the Super-Objective

Stanislavski defined the "super-objective" as the core motive and inspiration of the author. Whereas the subtext focuses on the author's meaning, the super-objective focuses on the author's motive. If the Bible's subtext is that, "God is good," then the Bible's super-objective is, "God is love." Love is God's motive - - always. "God is love." 1 Jn. 4:8. **"For God so loved the world, that he gave his only begotten Son, that whosoever believeth in him should not perish, but have everlasting life."** Jn. 3:16. Amazingly, Stanislavski said that an actor cannot reach the super-objective by the mind alone. It requires "complete surrender, passionate desire and unequivocal action." As we surrender fully to God in this moment, this allows the Holy Spirit to work within us "to will and to do," to passionately desire and unequivocally act to fulfill the will of God by pure-hearted performance. This is the perfect description of the state of certainty found only in *The Jesus Mood*. This is the imperative mood - - complete surrender to Christ, passionate desire from Christ and unequivocal action through Christ. And this is all found only from finding and cleaving to the Bible's super-objective - - GOD IS LOVE!

Directed Attention Key #5 -
Incarnate the Character

The Word becomes flesh in us. We study it. Recite it. Meditate it. Rehearse it. Confess it. Become it. The nature of God becomes so real to us that we can taste it. We taste it. We internalize it. We digest it fully. This is what communion is - - partaking of the image of Christ, faith to faith and glory to glory. **"But we all, with open face beholding as in a glass the glory of the Lord, are changed into the same image from glory to glory, even as by the Spirit of the Lord."** 2 Cor. 3:18. This is our glorious destiny - - to recognize, realize and release the divine nature of Christ Who indwells us mightily. **"For whom he did foreknow, he also did predestinate to be conformed to the image of his Son, that he might be the firstborn among many brethren."** Rom. 8:29. When we see Him, we shall be like Him. **"Beloved, now are we the sons of God, and it doth not yet appear what we shall be: but we know that, when he shall appear, we shall be like him; for we shall see him as he is."** 1 Jn. 3:2. Change from within enables greater vision without - - vision which sees God in all things, sees hope for all things and sees the salvation of all things. Stanislavski said that an actor must die in his character and a director must die in his actors. Die to self, in other words. When we die to self, then we incarnate the character of Christ. Jesus is our Divine Director who died for us that He could live in us as we die to ourselves so that we can live within Him. **"I am crucified with Christ: nevertheless I live; yet not I, but Christ liveth in me: and the life which I now live in the flesh I live by the faith of the Son of God, who loved me, and gave himself for me."** Gal. 2:20.

Directed Attention Key #6 -
Maintain the Line of Action in Each Scene

The line of action is the term Stanislavski used to describe the flow of the play's events toward the accomplishment of the super-objective. The line of action galvanizes all the small events, units and objectives of a character's life and directs them toward the climax of the play where the super-objective is accomplished. For the Christian, as we stay in the character of Christ, growing in and with Him, then the Holy Spirit galvanizes every scene of our lives to further the revelation of the super-objective, "God is love." Every scene of our life matters. Nothing is trivial. Nothing is pointless. If we stay in character. In Christ, every event of our lives helps to usher into this world the manifest love of God. Every conversation with our children. Every touch with our spouse. Every encounter with another is a spiritual scene of potential written from the beginning of time by the author and finisher of our faith. Every comb of the hair, morning shower, drive to work and simple chore becomes high romance with the Lord and love of our life as we maintain the line of action. Every gesture, word, thought and act helps momentum manifest toward the restoration and reconciliation of all things to Christ. **"For this cause we also, since the day we heard it, do not cease to pray for you, and to desire that ye might be filled with the knowledge of his will in all wisdom and spiritual understanding; That ye might walk worthy of the Lord unto all pleasing, being fruitful in every good work, and increasing in the knowledge of God; Strengthened with all might, according to his glorious power, unto all patience and longsuffering with joyfulness; Giving thanks unto the Father, which hath made us meet to be partakers of the inheritance of the saints in light: Who hath delivered us from the power of darkness, and hath translated us into the kingdom of his dear Son: In whom we have redemption through his blood, even the forgiveness of sins: Who is the image of the invisible God, the** firstborn of every creature: For by him were all things created, that are in heaven, and that are in earth, visible and invisible, whether they be thrones, or dominions, or principalities, or powers: all things were created by him, and for him: and he is before all things, and by him all things consist. And he is the head of the body, the church: who is the beginning, the firstborn from the dead; that in all things he might have the preeminence. For it pleased the Father that in him should all fullness dwell; and, having made peace through the blood of his cross, by him to reconcile all things unto himself; by him, I say, whether they be things in earth, or things in heaven. . . .Whereof I am made a minister, according to the dispensation of God which is given to me for you, to fulfill the word of God; Even the mystery which hath been hid from ages and from generations, but now is made manifest to his saints: To whom God would make known what is the riches of the glory of this mystery among the Gentiles; which is Christ in you, the hope of glory." Col. 1:9-20, 25-27.

Directed Attention Key #7 - *Today, Here, Now!*

This was Stanislavski's great truth - - today, here, now. Present yourself to the present. Be fully here. Then you can fully hear. Take no thought for tomorrow or yesterday. Today is the day of salvation - - always today. The Israelites were given supernatural provision - - one day at a time. Manna was given for today, here and now. It would become rotten if the Israelites tried to horde it up for tomorrow. God doesn't give tomorrow's manna today. Today's manna is never to be found in yesterday's pot. God's presence is always in the present. You must learn to present yourself to the present. Ground yourself in the "now." Anchor yourself in the "near." Bathe yourself in the "new." These are the dynamics of God - - Immanuel is God <u>near</u> us, Yahweh is God who <u>now</u> is, and Jesus is God who makes all things <u>new</u> (Is. 7:14; Ex. 3:14; 2 Cor. 5:17). Monitor your thoughts, ideas, emotions continually and allow no fear of tomorrow or hurt of yesterday to divert your focus. God is in the now. Your destiny is in the now. Love is now. Faith is now. The past completed work of the Cross has established all of our "nows" in righteousness, peace and joy in the Holy Spirit. This is the Kingdom of God (Rom. 14:17). Scriptures tell us to be "instant" with our faith at all times (Rom. 12:12; 2 Tim. 4:2). This speaks of spontaneous readiness to act quickly and decisively in the now. No paralysis of analysis, but instead alertness to bolt into action. As Smith Wigglesworth famously said, "I'm on the plan of daring, <u>acting</u> in the Holy Spirit." The Holy Spirit is our eternal helper and motivator. Direct your attention on the Spirit and you will never regret it. **"God is our refuge and strength, a very present help in trouble."** Ps. 46:1. God is not just "present." He is "very present." A very present "help" - - today, here and now!

Gutsy Performance

Actors and athletes are complimented from time to time as giving "gutsy" or "gut-wrenching" efforts. I like this reference to the "gut." I think the gut-realm is largely ignored by Christians, ignorance which obviously results in "gutless" faith. Jesus said that our belly is the source of our spiritual life. **"He that believeth on me, as the scripture hath said, out of his belly shall flow rivers of living water."** Jn. 7:38. In this verse, the Greek word for "belly" is "koilia" and means the womb, stomach and innermost being. Interestingly, koilia is the basis for the Latin word for "Heaven," which is "coelum." Thus, Heaven's touch point in us resides in our "gut."

In the Old Testament, the "gut" was the spiritual center of man. The King James translates this area as "reins," which in the Hebrew is "kilyah" and literally means "kidneys." Biblical scholar Marvin Wilson notes that the Jews believed "the seat of the will, emotions, mind and spiritual powers is often found in the general area of the gastro-intestinal tract." More specifically, the kidneys represented both the physical and spiritual center of man. Even in animals, the kidneys and blood were not eaten because they represented the spiritual life of the animal and thus were sacred as belonging only to God (Lev. 3:10-11; 17:11). Consider the following verses:

> **"The spirit of man is the candle of the LORD, searching all the inward parts of the belly."** Prov. 20:27.

> **"I will bless the LORD, who hath given me counsel: my reins also instruct me in the night seasons."** Ps. 16:7.

> **"Examine me, O LORD, and prove me; try my reins and my heart."** Ps. 26:2.

> **"Thou hast planted them, yea, they have taken root: they grow, yea, they bring forth fruit: thou art near in their mouth, and far from their reins."** Jer. 12:2.

When King David said in Psalm 51:6 that God "desirest truth in the inward parts," "inward parts" is the translation of the Hebrew word "tuwchah" which is another word for "kidney." Tuwchah derives from "tachah," which means "to stretch a bow as an archer." Thus, our gut here is pictured as a bow which launches truth from the center of our being. "Then said I (David), Lo, I come: in the volume of the book it is written of me, I delight to do thy will, O my God: yea, thy law is <u>within</u> <u>my</u> <u>heart</u>" (literally "in the midst of my bowels"). Ps. 40:7-8. David lived out of his gut, and so can we. As we "go with our gut," we will discover new levels of passion and intensity.

Likewise, the New Testament also stresses the importance of the gut\belly\kidneys\reins. Jesus "searcheth the reins and hearts" of all men (Rev. 2:23). The Greek word for reins is "nephros," which again literally means "kidneys." Greek scholar W. E. Vine states, "The will and affections were regarded as having their seat in kidneys." Colossians 3:12 instructs us to "put on . . . as the elect of God . . . bowels of mercies." The Greek word for "bowels" in this passage is "splanchna," which W. E. Vine says represents the seat of passions for the Greek and the seat of tender affections for the Hebrew. When Jesus was "moved with compassion" toward the multitude and "He healed their sick," "splanchnizomai" is the verb used to describe Jesus' action (Matt. 14:14). Splanchnizomai, the verb form of splanchna (bowels), means to be moved to action by one's bowels or inward parts. Jesus, in other words, was moved by His gut, led by His gut and empowered by His gut. Jesus wants us to have this same "gut-life," and He promised that rivers of living water would flow out of our bellies (Jn. 7:38).

When Romans 8:5-6 contrasts the terms "carnally minded" and "spiritually minded," the Greek word for "minded" comes from the root "phren" which translates as "midriff" or "abdomen." Thus, when we are told to "mind the things of the spirit" or to be "spiritually minded," the more accurate sense of this is to be "spiritually gutsy" or to "set our gut on the things of the spirit." The exact same Greek word is translated as "affection" in the following verse: "Set your affection (gut) on things above, not on things on the earth" (Col. 3:2). This same word is translated as "savourest" in Matthew 16:23 where Jesus describes Satan's evil as that state of being which "savourest not" the things that be of God. Satan, in other words, has no gut-desire for God. Scriptures cry out for us to set our guts on things above, on the spirit within and on all the things of God. What a visceral intensity this adds to our spiritual walk! Great actors have this gutsiness. Great athletes have this gutsiness. And great Christians have this gutsiness.

The appreciation of the human gut has a long and distinguished history as well as an ever growing place in science and medicine. In history, the human gut\reins\bowels has a key place in all Eastern countries. These cultures revere the gut as the source of "chi," which refers to the life force or vital energy of life. In China, this concept is called "qi" or "chi" and in Korea and Japan it is called "ki." Chinese, Korean and Japanese ideas regarding the chi are nearly identical. The Indian term, "prana" or "pranja," has the same connection to the idea of the spirit. This life force is located in the abdomen (the "hara") where it is controlled by the breath. It is thought that one's chi can be seen in one's personality, and in all outward actions and that it is more powerful than physical strength alone. It is considered a reflection of the inner person. Strong chi is therefore the equivalent of good character. Chi is an important concept in Asian philosophies that underlie all martial arts. I am not touting Eastern philosophy at all because it is entirely lacking in the saving knowledge of Jesus Christ. But, they, along with the Israelites and Greeks, have identified the true center of human spirituality - - the gut.

Science has now discovered that the human gut is indeed what Webster's says it is: "the basic visceral or emotional part of a person." The gut actually has its own brain which forms the enteric nervous system while staying connected to the central nervous system and the other brain encased in our skulls. In the book *The Second Brain*, Dr. Michael Gershon reports that there are a hundred million neurotransmitters which line the gut, the same approximate number found in the brain. It appears that our capacity for feeling and emotional expression depends primarily on the gut and, to a lesser extent, the brain. Gershon says, "the gut may be more intellectual than the heart and may have a greater capacity for feeling." Several mood enhancing chemicals appear to be released through the gut's neurotransmitters. The gut still remains largely a mystery to science and medicine, yet its importance is progressively being revealed and established.

The coin of the realm for the spiritual warrior is strength and courage. Every Christian needs a "gut check" for these two treasures. Without strength and courage burning in our belly, our faith walk is weak-kneed and lily-livered. Three times in Joshua 1 the Lord exhorted His people to be strong and courageous as they stormed the Promised Land. The Apostle Paul gives us like charge: "Be on the alert, stand firm in the faith, act like men, be strong" (1 Cor. 16:13). Just as atoms are brought together in violent collision to produce nuclear power, so are strength and courage the twin dynamos that energize our faith to overcome the world. Most men's gut-life has been locked away in a dungeon of weak and passion-less "religion." It is time we all get re-acquainted with our guts - - gut-power, gut-leading and gut-passion.

I mourn when I hear Christians talk about God or pray to God in gutless tones and feeble terms. People far too often dis-play the same intensity toward God as they do when ordering fast-food through an automated drive-through machine. The living God deserves all our intensity and gut-desire. Nothing about God is routine, ordinary and matter-of-fact. Our voic-es should be amplified with awe and adoration whenever we talk to or about God. Our tones should <u>never</u> be plastic, le-thargic or lukewarm when it comes to God - - never!

Something is missing in the faith that is preached today. We are taught that faith is mental agreement with the Word of God. We keep agreeing, yet keep losing the daily battles with Satan. The missing element is in the realm of the gut. Here the battle of faith is truly fought.

Mere mental assent is just wishing and takes no strength or courage. Gut assent is deepest desire ignited by all the strength and courage a Christian can muster. A.W. Tozer said, "It may be said without qualification that every man is as holy and as full of the Spirit as he wants to be. He may not be as full as he wishes he were, but he is most certainly as full as he wants to be." True faith is born in the bowels of passionate "wanting" rather than the stagnant waters of mental "wishing."

The Jews believed the deepest affections of man were re-lated to the area of the kidneys and bowels. The King James translates this place as the "reins" (Ps. 7:9). The New Ameri-can Standard translates this area as the "inward parts" (Ps. 139:13) and "inmost being" (Pr. 23:16). Common sense translates this word as "guts." Jesus confirmed this when He said, "He that believeth on me, as the scripture hath said, out of his belly shall flow rivers of living water." (Jn. 7:38 KJV). *Foxe's Book of Martyrs* describes "stoutness of stomach" as a key quality of spiritual champions. Let every Christian seize this same stoutness of gut in the battle against evil.

Legendary Olympic runner Steve Prefontaine said, "A lot of people run a race to see who's the fastest. I run to see who has the most guts." Prefontaine understood the currency of true competition is not ability, but inner desire. Spiritually, God also values guts above ability for "the race is not to the swift" (Eccl. 9:11). The spiritual "race" is won with gut wrenching "endurance" that refuses to "lose heart" (Heb. 12:1-4).

Disraeli said, "Man is only truly great when he acts from the passions." Let every Christian aspire to passionate greatness in the service of our Lord. Men feel the most alive and are the most successful when their guts are on fire. This holds true in war, sports and love. True passion flows from the belly in the form of excitement, desire and effort. Value strength and courage as the fuel of faith which puts lightning in your belly and victory in your life. Remember, spiritual strength plus spiritual courage equals spiritual guts. Solve the equation now by fervently seeking God for this blessing. "On the day I called Thou didst answer me; Thou didst make me bold with strength in my soul." Ps. 138:3. Just as actors need their guts to get into full character, so do we need our guts to get into the full character of Christ. I know Stanislavski would agree.

Getting In New Testament Character

The concept of communion is our call to daily remembrance to incarnate the Spirit of Christ Who indwells us (1 Cor. 11:23-26). We are called to spiritually eat the flesh and drink the blood of Christ. **"Then Jesus said unto them, Verily, verily, I say unto you, Except ye eat the flesh of the Son of man, and drink his blood, ye have no life in you. Whoso eateth my flesh, and drinketh my blood, hath eternal life; and I will raise him up at the last day. For my flesh is meat indeed, and my blood is drink indeed. He that eateth my flesh, and drinketh my blood, dwelleth in me, and I in him. As the living Father hath sent me, and I live by the Father: so he that eateth me, even he shall live by me. This is that bread which came down from heaven: not as your fathers did eat manna, and are dead: he that eateth of this bread shall live for ever."** Jn. 6:53-58.

What does it mean to eat Jesus' flesh and drink His blood? It means to consume His motive, mood and mind. We are called to be "partakers of the divine nature of Christ" (2 Pet. 1:4). The divine nature of Christ means just what it says - - the very thoughts, passions and strengths of our Lord. We are to consume them, digest them and incarnate them.

Jesus came not only to substitute His death for our death, but He also came to substitute His life for our life (Gal. 2:20; Col. 3:3-4). Thus, in the most literal sense, we have complete access to the full mind, heart, personality, gifting, strength and anointing of Jesus. This understanding unlocks the mystery of ministering in Jesus' name. John 14:12-14 promises believers we will do the same and greater works than Jesus did and that He will do whatever we ask in His name. Yet, billions of literal prayers in Jesus' name have failed. Why? Because ministering the name of Jesus means far more than just reciting His proper name. This is where "the Method" comes into play. Before we can use the name of Jesus, we must first incarnate the name. Before we can incarnate the name, we need to first understand what the name represents.

For the Hebrew, the "name" represents the character or nature of a person. The name is far more than what one is called. It is the fullness of who one is - - in character, nature, authority and strength. Ministering Jesus' name means ministering His Divine Nature into the situation at hand. But, the key to this revelation is this: we don't minister Jesus' Divine Nature down from Heaven; instead, we minister Jesus' Divine Nature out of ourselves. This is why Christ in us is the hope of glory, not Christ outside of us (Col. 1:27). All we have to do to access God's Divine Nature is to "believe on the name (nature) of His Son Jesus Christ, and love one another, as He gave us commandment. And he that keepeth his commandments dwelleth in him, and he in him. And hereby we know that he abideth in us, by the Spirit which he hath given us" (1 Jn. 3:23-24). Believing on Jesus Christ does not mean believing on Jesus being separate and apart from you. No, believing on Jesus is trusting that Christ now indwells you and is ready, willing and able to take over any situation you confidently and aggressively yield to Him. You minister in His name as you release out of you His Divine Nature, which is the wisdom and power of God.

Do you see this great truth? New Testament communion is "putting on" the name and character of Jesus Christ (Rom. 13:14). We are all called to be actors of "the ultimate Method" - - putting on the mind of Christ (1 Cor. 2:16), putting on the personal armor of Jesus (Eph. 6:10-17) and putting on the Son of God's wisdom, righteousness, sanctification and redemption (1 Cor. 1:30). "Putting on Jesus" means performing the Word in spirit and truth. Jesus is the Word. Believe Him. Belove Him. Bespeak Him. Behold Him. This is "the Method" of faith which will perform *The Jesus Mood* brilliantly on the stages of all our lives.

Chapter 6
The Tree of Life

In Chapter One, I presented you with an idea that will change your life forever - - that *The Jesus Mood* lives in you, a mood which gives you perfect confidence <u>in</u> God and imperative authority <u>from</u> God to reconcile all reality <u>to</u> God. In Chapter Two, I shared the foundation on which *The Jesus Mood* rests - - the "always already" past completed work of the Cross, which has always already healed us, always already saved us and always already delivered us from all evil. In Chapter Three, "Duality" was revealed as the mother of all mood-killers, the root source of the deadly *Tree of the Knowledge of Good and Evil* and the ultimate way we neglect our so great a salvation. In Chapter Four, "Plenitude" shone forth as the blessed mindset locked and loaded on the Lord's fullness in all things. In Chapter Five, "performing the Word" was seen as "the Method" of internal focus which allows us to incarnate the mood, mind and motive of Christ in all our ways. This final chapter ties all these dynamics up into one glorious concept - - the *Tree of Life.*

The Jesus Mood is the *Tree of Life.* We are back in the Garden. We have full access to this tree of trees. We are no longer ignorant of the *Tree of the Knowledge of Good and Evil.* Through mistake, agony, failure and death, we have learned this tree all too well. But, the curse has been reversed. Jesus died so that we could be re-rooted and re-grafted back onto the *Tree of Life.* He was crucified <u>to</u> death on the *Tree of the Knowledge of Good and Evil* so that we could be resurrected <u>from</u> death back onto the *Tree of Life.*

Adam was called to abide in *The Jesus Mood* as he took dominion of the Earth (Gen. 1:28). Adam forfeited that dominion to Satan. Jesus took it back at the Cross. Jesus then gave it back to us at Pentecost. Jesus now sits waiting for us to rise up in the imperative mood and start reconciling the visible world back to the invisible Kingdom of God.

Adam, before the fall, lived in the imperative mood. He ruled with his tongue. He named all the living creatures through the prophetic power of imperative speech. He didn't just arbitrarily pick a name out of a hat when he was naming all living things. No, he prophesied the God-given purpose over all creation. Adam's words galvanized creation to blossom forth its divine destiny. Nowhere is this dynamic better illustrated than in Adam's naming of Eve. In Matthew 19:4-6, Jesus clearly says that God spoke over Eve her divine purpose which was to be "one flesh" with her husband. Yet, Genesis 2:23-24 clearly says that Adam was the one to prophesy over Eve her divine purpose of being "one flesh" with him. How is this seeming contradiction resolved? Simple. <u>Both</u> God and Adam spoke in unison. Adam spoke only what he had already heard God speak. Adam's soul (mind and heart) then heard his own spirit (gut and conscience) reveal the Word of the Lord for Eve. God spoke to Eve through Adam's spirit. Adam's spirit heard God's Word for Eve. Adam's soul then consented to and spoke the same Word over Eve in the imperative mood. Adam, at this early stage, was a man <u>under</u> authority who could then speak <u>with</u> authority. Adam performed this same prophetic function over all living creation - - until the fall changed everything.

Today, dominion has been restored to us as the body of Christ (Eph. 1:22-23). We can now rule this world with our righteous confession. We are Kings upon the Earth called to reign in righteousness (Rev. 1:5-6). Jesus is the King of Kings by whom we are to reign (Rev. 19:16; Rom. 5:17). As righteous Kings, we are to rule with our confession. "A divine sentence is in the lips of the King: his mouth transgresseth not in judgment . . . .Righteous lips are the delight of Kings." Prov. 16:10,13. Scriptures tell us again and again that spoken words carry the power of life, death, salvation, miracles and deliverance (Prov. 18:21; Matt. 12:35-37; Rom. 10:8-10; Mk. 11:22-25; Ps. 107:20). "Where the word of a King is, there is power." Eccl. 8:4. A true warrior of God "dwelleth as a lion, and teareth the arm with the crown of the head" (Dt. 33:20). The imagery here is that a lion's "crown" is his "mouth." Your crown with which you tear Satan's arm is your mouth's kingly confession. This is the crown we will joyfully cast at the feet of Jesus as a sign of glorious submission.

What's the Big Idea?

As righteous Kings, we must understand the importance of ideas, words and moods. It all begins with an idea. An idea is a seed which we allow or disallow to be sown into our soul. If we allow the seed idea to be sown into our minds and hearts, it will spread its roots and grow. The more we care for, cultivate and refine the idea, the quicker and larger it will grow. Conversely, the less we care for, cultivate and refine the idea, the slower and smaller it will grow, if at all.

The Kingdom of God is an idea which is planted into us as a seed. **"And he said, So is the kingdom of God, as if a man should cast seed into the ground."** Mk. 4:26. The Kingdom itself is <u>not</u> a seed, however. It is finished and fully formed right now. But, for us in our fallen state, the <u>idea</u> of the Kingdom must begin as a seed. If we passionately care for this idea, if we diligently cultivate this idea and if we continually refine this idea by renewing our minds to its truth, <u>then</u> will the Kingdom of God manifest <u>from</u> idea <u>to</u> visible reality here on the Earth as it already manifests in Heaven.

Conversely, if we neglect this "idea" of God's Kingdom with our minds and hearts, then the reality of it wanes, our love wanes, our faith wanes, and our hope wanes. Though help is ever near, ever available and ever willing, our own neglect blocks the rescue. **"How shall we escape, if we neglect so great a salvation?"** Heb. 2:3. When Jesus traveled back to Nazareth in Mark 6:1-6, He was available for "mighty works," yet He "could there do no mighty work . . . . and He marveled because of their unbelief." In other words, Nazareth neglected the so great a salvation which appeared in their midst ready, willing, available and eager to bless them. They neglected the time of their visitation.

<u>This</u> is the day of <u>our</u> visitation, the seventh day visitation which lasts for eternity. There is no time when the Lord is not

visiting us. He is omni-present, ever present and fully present - - always. Only our neglect can keep His works from manifesting. Like Jesus at Nazareth, the Lord is always near us, in our hearts and mouths, ever ready to manifest mighty works, but we can still neglect to focus on Him with a believing heart, an expectant mind and a ready tongue. When this occurs, the Lord may marvel at our unbelief, but He doesn't leave, quit or disown us. He stays by our side, continually offering His mighty works on our behalf.

The key point is to avoid neglect. It is the only enemy which can defeat you. Only your neglect can block, hinder or obstruct the works of God. Satan, sin and oppression fill the vacuum our neglect creates. Conquer your neglect and nothing will ever defeat you.

Do you want to hear the cure for neglect? It is costly. Not in the realm of money, but in the realm of ideas. You must take each and every idea you have ever had and trade all of them for "the big idea." The "big idea" is both the pearl of great value and the treasure hidden in a field described in the following verses: **"Again, the kingdom of heaven is like unto treasure hid in a field; the which when a man hath found, he hideth, and for joy thereof goeth and selleth all that he hath, and buyeth that field. Again, the kingdom of heaven is like unto a merchant man, seeking goodly pearls: Who, when he had found one pearl of great price, went and sold all that he had, and bought it."** Matt. 13:44-46. Do you see the common theme? Both men so valued the hidden treasure and the pearl of great price, that they were willing to sell everything that they had previously valued.

Jesus used these examples to explain the cost of the Kingdom of God. It doesn't cost money, but it costs ideas. Whatever ideas you have valued in your own righteousness must be exchanged for the single big idea of the Kingdom of God.

Your faith follows your ideas. Whatever ideas you esteem with your thoughts and emotions will determine what you are believing on and in. Let's consider some illustrations. The rich young ruler sorrowfully rejected Jesus' call not because he had great possessions, but rather because the "idea" of great possessions was bigger and more esteemed by him than was the "idea" of God's calling. Do you see? Satan didn't bribe Adam and Eve with "actual booty," but rather with the "idea of booty." Fear is an "idea" we buy into. We emotionally invest into fear by fretting. We mentally invest into fear with racing thoughts of dreaded outcomes. We physically invest into fear with poor posture, hypertension and panicked countenances. The "idea" draws our focus. Our focus develops our belief. Our belief produces fruit. That fruit can be rotten. That fruit can be deadly. However, if the "idea" is the Kingdom of God, then the fruit will be blessed.

Beloved, "despair" is nothing more than an idea. But, as we accept, cultivate and invest our thoughts and emotions into this idea, it grows deeper and larger into our being. We even start "tithing" our first focus and best effort toward the idea of despair. We process all things through its lens of lack. Our gloomy confessions come into line with it and we are snared. This idea has become a stronghold and we are now prisoners to this demonic despair. Repentance is the rejection of wrong ideas in favor of the one right idea. Just as the merchant sold all his previous "ideas" of riches in exchange for the pearl of great value, repentance is our way of selling off any and all fleshly ideas which wrongly possess or divert our heart. Consider the following verses on this point: **"For godly sorrow worketh repentance to salvation not to be repented of: but the sorrow of the world worketh death. For behold this selfsame thing, that ye sorrowed after a godly sort, what carefulness it wrought in you, yea, what clearing of yourselves, yea, what indignation, yea, what fear, yea, what vehement desire, yea, what zeal, yea, what revenge! In all things ye have approved yourselves to be clear in this matter."** 2 Cor. 7:10-11.

So, <u>how</u> do we sell each and every idea in exchange for the one big idea of the Kingdom of God? We repent! The Greek word for "repentance" is "metanoia" and literally means "to change the way of thinking." In other words, we repent when we get rid of ideas which have risen up against us fully knowing and trusting God. As the previously quoted passage suggests, this takes "carefulness" in monitoring our thought life, a "clearing" away of wrong ideas, as well as righteous "anger" toward fleshly thinking, "zealous" focus to remain single-eyed on the Kingdom of God, and a willingness to hunt down and execute "revenge" on any rebellious thought or emotion of unbelief running around in our minds and hearts. In our thought life, we must take no prisoners. All rebellious thoughts must be immediately captured and executed. **"For though we walk in the flesh, we do not war after the flesh: (For the weapons of our warfare are not carnal, but mighty through God to the pulling down of strong holds;) Casting down imaginations, and every high thing that exalteth itself against the knowledge of God, and bringing into captivity every thought to the obedience of Christ; and having in a readiness to revenge all disobedience, when your obedience is fulfilled."** 2 Cor. 10:3-6.

It's important to understand the various sources of ideas. An idea can originate from me, or from the demonic realm, from other individual men, or from the corporate consciousness of fallen man. When Cain slew Abel, he was the first to have the "idea" of murder. That idea then spread into the collective consciousness of all men and nations. War and violence is now a part of our collective psyche. We live with violent thoughts, violent emotions, and violent words. While all men may not have committed murder, all men share the common idea of anger toward one another, which Jesus said is the root idea of murder (Matt. 5:21-22). Satan no doubt helped this idea first germinate in Cain. Do you see? It's like second-hand smoke. I may not smoke myself, but if I inhale the smoke of other nearby smokers I can die from its toxic effects. Similarly, I may not originate an idea of lust, murder, hatred, jealousy or dishonesty; but I can still be infected with the toxic effects of the idea if I take it into my heart and mind. This is why what you watch and who you listen to is so important. If you continually expose yourself to images, people and situations which are driven by toxic ideas, then this "smoke" can infect your thinking. Many of our ideas are self-generated, but most are the second-hand smoke of others' toxic mindsets. Add to these dynamics demonic influence, and the battlefield is now revealed. The battle of life is fought on the field of ideas. The idea we focus on the most is the idea which will grow and bear fruit. Guard your heart from your own fleshly ideas. Guard your heart from the ideas of other fleshly men. Guard your heart from corporate ideas of racism, nationalism and institutionalism, etc. Guard your heart from Satan. Cleave to the one big idea of God - - "Jesus saves!"

When I was younger, I let the "idea" of "lust" take root in

my being. It grew like kudzu, taking over all my thoughts, emotions and energies. When the Lord delivered me of lust, He sent me a stronger "idea," one that will never leave me. It was a dream. In this dream, I was a little child lost on a filthy city street full of prostitutes, bars and pornographic businesses. I was crying and so scared. Then a huge hand grabbed me and pulled me over to the other side of the street where it was clean and safe. It was the softest yet strongest hand I had ever felt. I looked up and beheld a nine foot tall black man with pink light coming out of his eyes. I knew I was safe - - completely safe. The dream ended. This prophetic idea birthed my deliverance from lust. I knew God's will was to save me from this evil desire. Whether the man in my dream was God or an angel from God, I know not. But I know the idea of my dream was God's promise to me of deliverance. I love God so much.

Lust was evicted from my life by the power of God. When I received the idea, the power was then able to begin manifesting the deliverance of God. But as I was delivered, the Lord sent me yet another prophetic image - - the jawbone of Samson. The mighty Samson picked up the fresh jawbone of an ass in Judges 15 and used it as a smashing weapon to kill a thousand Philistine soldiers. The Lord showed me that in Christ I had the spiritual strength of Samson, but that my jawbone was to be my righteous confessions which I brandish against my spiritual enemies. The Lord led me to take "vengeance" on lustful thoughts by imagining myself picking up the jawbone of faith and bashing in the heads of all lewd and tempting thoughts. It works - - guaranteed.

The handful of times over the last twenty years that I neglected to take vengeance on attacking thoughts, the idea of

lust returned to buffet me. But as soon as I repented and re-
focused on the big idea, the lustful thoughts were executed,
burned and their ashes scattered. Hallelujah! I can say with
assurance that the only time my deliverance is ever chal-
lenged is when I neglect to focus on it.

Life and Logos

Now, let's consider the sources of all ideas. There are only
two - - the *Tree of the Knowledge of Good and Evil* and the
Tree of Life. We have already studied the former tree throughout this book in the earlier passages on Lackitude and Duality. I now want to focus on the *Tree of Life* and its ideas.
God's ideas all come from the *Tree of Life*. God's ideas are
perfect, powerful and pure.

I want you to visualize the *Tree of Life* with a wide and deep
root system and a thick and mighty trunk which supports a
vast number of fruitful branches. I want to call the tree itself
the "Logos." The fertile seed-filled fruit off of the tree I want
to call the "Rhema."

Let's study these two words. Logos is a Greek term meaning
"word," which is defined as "an expression of a thought."
Logos, in other words, is an expressed idea. But, not just <u>an</u>
idea, but <u>the</u> idea. Logos is the special expression of an idea
which conveys the essence or nature of the thinker. For example, Jesus is called "the Logos" in John 1:1,12,14 (translated as "Word"). Jesus is not just an expressed idea <u>about</u>
God, but He is the expressed idea <u>of</u> God which reveals the
essence, character, person and nature of God.

*"In the beginning was the Word (Logos), and the Word (Lo-
gos) was with God, and the Word (Logos) was God. The*

same was in the beginning with God. All things were made by Him; and without Him was not anything made that was made. In Him was life; and the life was the light of men . . . . and the Word (Logos) was made flesh, and dwelt among us, (and we beheld His glory, the glory as of the only begotten of the Father,) full of grace and truth . . . . But as many as received Him, to them gave He power to become the sons of God, even to them that believe on His name." Jn. 1:1-4,14,12.

What a passage! It tells us that Jesus is <u>the</u> eternal Logos <u>of</u> God Who has always been <u>with</u> God and in fact <u>is</u> God. All things were made by, for and through Jesus as the Logos. Thus, Jesus reveals the essence of God. This essence of God put on human flesh and dwelt among us, allowing us to behold His glory as the <u>only</u> begotten of the Father. Better yet, we weren't just allowed to behold Him, but He also gave us who believe in Him "power to become the sons of God."

The power for us to become sons of God resides solely in the Logos. Jesus is God's big idea. This idea drenches all reality with the glory of the only begotten Son. As we receive, refine and realize the Logos, the glory <u>manifests</u> in and around us in greater and greater degree and intensity.

It all begins with the idea. The idea of the Logos must be sown and received into our hearts. If we have "an honest and good heart" in hearing the Word and <u>then</u> we "keep it, and bring forth fruit with patience," then we will find "perfection" (Lk. 8:14-15).

The Gospel <u>is</u> the Logos. The Gospel <u>is</u> a seed. The Gospel <u>is</u> an idea. The Gospel <u>is</u> Jesus. As the Gospel grows in our hearts, the idea of Jesus grows - - the essence of Jesus grows - - the fruit of Jesus grows. You cannot separate the idea of Jesus from the essence of Jesus. You cannot separate the essence of Jesus from the presence of Jesus. You cannot separate the presence of Jesus from the Logos of God.

The key in all of this is to continually allow the *idea\seed\Logos* to be refined within your heart - - and refined, and refined and refined and refined. Constant "day and night" care must be given the *idea\seed\Logos* that it "should spring and grow up" until "the harvest is come" (Mk. 4:26-29). On the other hand, if we neglect to refine the *idea\seed\Logos*, then the cares of the world will choke the fruit of the Word from manifesting.

Albert Einstein once said, "Make things as simple as possible, but not simpler." I believe that the primary reason the Gospel is not displayed in greater power today is that most Christians have over-simplified the *idea\seed\Logos*. Christians speak of God's goodness but still believe He sends destructions, diseases and disasters. They never allow this contradiction to be refined of impurity and error. Christians believe God promises to help us in time of need, yet have nothing but shoulder shrugs when trying to give an answer as to why deliverance rarely comes to Christians suffering with cancer, divorce, depression or other disaster. Many Christians have over-simplified the Gospel into one big shoulder shrug which says, "We don't understand God's will in this life, but we will one day when we reach Heaven." This is making the Gospel simpler than possible.

Martial arts legend Bruce Lee once talked about the simplicity of the fist. When he first studied the fist, he thought, "A fist is just a fist." But, as he studied the fist in greater degree, he began to notice all of the intricate bone structures, multiple angles and complex movements possible. He saw that the fist was wonderfully and amazingly complicated beyond anything he had ever previously studied. Over the following years, he learned all there was to know about the fist. Then, one day he had an epiphany - - "A fist is just a fist." Lee had crossed the field of complexity to return to simplicity. Had he never studied and refined his understanding of the fist, he would still be in the over-simplified mindset that, "A fist is just a fist." He could answer no questions about the fist in this mindset because he had obtained no depth of understanding. But, after refining his understanding through "night and day" cultivation of the idea of the fist, he was able to obtain the right kind of simplicity with true depth of understanding and appreciation of the magnificent statement, "A fist is just a fist."

When I first attended law school, I thought we were going to just memorize law. I thought law school was about learning the law. Boy, was I wrong. Law school is about learning to read analytically, think critically and speak confidently. You can have every jot and tittle of the law memorized, but still have no clue how to understand, apply and vigorously debate its meaning. Only by dissecting the law from every angle and then putting it back together can we properly appreciate and apply it. A law can only be profoundly simple after it has been profoundly studied.

"Jesus saves" is a wonderfully simple statement, but we must all cross the field of complexity to understand the true meaning of its simplicity. "Jesus saves" means little to me until I understand its scope, application and implications for my life. If I remain clueless or unconvinced as to the limitless application of these two wonderful words, "Jesus saves," then I will spend my life shoulder shrugging all my failures and disappointments away.

This also explains why many Christians appear shallow, judgmental and narrow minded to the rest of the world. We give robotically rote answers, sermons and teachings over and over and over again. We memorize exact mechanical phrases to speak to the world. The Gospel has been reduced in many people's minds to a canned presentation similar in form to any salesman peddling products. In other words, the Gospel has been grossly over-simplified.

This is not the Logos! As we <u>refine</u> the idea "Jesus saves" into every fiber of our being, something wonderful happens. We become fully persuaded and gloriously convinced that "Jesus saves" applies to everything in our lives. Everything. Everything! It applies to our thought life, our emotional life, our physical life, our social life, our financial life and our family life. Only as we allow full refinement of God's big idea will it manifest into this earthly realm.

The Logos is the root, trunk and branches of the wonderful *Tree of Life*. The Rhema is the seed-filled fruit which drops off the *Tree of Life* to spread that life to other heart soils. Simply put, Logos is the big idea of God which is Jesus Christ, while Rhema is the specific application of that big idea to a particular situation at a particular time.

Rhema comes from the Greek word "rheo" which means "to flow." Rhema itself is defined as "a spoken word." The Rhema of God is a word spoken by the Logos to our "now" situation. Again, the Logos is the *Tree of Life* while the Rhema is the life-giving seed-filled fruit off of that tree. Let's consider two key passages on this point: "Let the Word (Logos) dwell in you richly." Col. 3:16. This passage describes the indwelling Jesus Who lives in us as the Logos of God. "Man shall not live by bread alone, but by every Word (Rhema) of God." Lk. 4:4. We are to walk in the continual hearing of God's specific Words spoken to us for each and every life situation we encounter. The Logos is the ocean of Jesus' essence, while the Rhemas are the rivers that flow that essence to our current situation and present awareness. Again, Logos is the big idea of "Jesus saves" which covers everything, while the Rhema is the specific and particularized word spoken by the Logos to our "now" need. Simply put, Logos is what and who Jesus is, while Rhema is what Jesus specifically speaks and commands.

Never forget this one thing: you cannot cause God to act. Your prayers don't cause God to act. Your righteousness doesn't cause God to act. Your travailing in agony doesn't cause God to act. In fact, whenever we think we can cause God to act, we are actually dishonoring God. We think He has left something undone, or that His future works toward us are somehow conditional on what we do. No! God has already acted. GOD HAS ALREADY ACTED! Fully, finally and decisively. God has pre-responded in the Heavenly realm and pre-provided all His works of deliverance and loving kindness toward us and for us. God is always ahead of us - - light years ahead of us. We don't wait on Him to act. He already has. He waits on us to act in faith based on what He has already accomplished. This is why we can be "certain" of God's deliverances - - because they have already been completed from God's perspective. All we do, and I do mean all, is pay attention and consent to what the Spirit says God has already done. This act of consent releases the completed work of Christ to visibly manifest in this earthly realm.

We are only really capable of two responses in this life. We can pay our tithe of attention to the unseen Kingdom of God and consent to its provisions, <u>or</u> we can neglect our so great a total salvation and thereby deny its provision. Pay attention and consent. Neglect and deny. It's that simple. The question is <u>not</u> whether <u>God</u> will or will not act. Rather the question <u>is</u> whether or not <u>we</u> will act by heeding and consenting to the past completed work of the Cross. The key to certainty is not to be convinced about the future. That will always be impossible. Rather, we are to be convinced about the past. Our goal is to bring the past into the manifest present. A certain present has to be based on a certain past. The past completed work of Christ is the Logos - - the eternal idea and essence of God. The manifest present is the Rhema - - the imperative consent and command of God's wisdom and provision into the "now" situation. This is *The Jesus Mood* - - our consent <u>to</u> and then command <u>of</u> the works of God. "If ye abide in me, and my words (Rhemas) abide in you, ye shall ask (demand by speaking) what ye will, and it shall be done unto you." Jn. 15:7. This is the "effectual fervent prayer of a righteous man" which "availeth much" (Jas. 5:16).

Pray This Way

So, what exactly is prayer? How did Jesus pray? How do we pray? How do we pray without ceasing? How does confessing Scriptures relate to prayer? In what sense is prayer perfect speech?

First, prayer is interaction with God. Participation in each other's presence. Fellowship. Worship. Friendship. Awe. Communion. Intimacy. Union. Our souls' fluid and spontaneous flow with God's indwelling Spirit. This place of inner-dialogue with the Lord takes place in the human heart. It is the heart we are to guard with all diligence for from it flow the "issues" (literally "deliverances") of life (Prov. 4:23). God is always searching the hearts of men, seeking to help us unite and enlarge our hearts with His love (1 Chr. 28:9; 2 Chr. 16:9; Ps. 86:11; 119:32; Heb. 4:12). Interestingly, one of the New Testament words for "prayer" translated as "intercessions" in 1 Timothy 2:1 is "enteuxis" and literally means "to interview or confer with." Prayer is conferencing with God in the chambers of the heart.

Prayer does not originate on the tongue but in the heart. It is primarily non-verbal and consists of tender touches and powerful promptings of faith, hope and love - - all ministered within our hearts by the wonderful Holy Spirit. These touches must be hungered for, hoped for and listened for, or else they are not felt or recognized. Neglecting the Holy Spirit's inner-witness is the source of all failure, unbelief and hardness of heart. Heart-prayer is the cure for all failure, unbelief and hardness of heart - - it's that simple. In fact, when Scriptures instruct us to pray without ceasing, they are not referring to verbal prayer but to heart-prayer. We can't <u>verbally</u> pray 24/7, but we can always pitch our hearts toward God.

This is the life of prayer, to abide in continual and spontaneous receptivity to the Holy Spirit. This spiritual sensitivity is all in the Book of Acts, and it is oh so available for us as well. Stop viewing prayer as oral communication <u>with</u> God. Rather, view prayer as oral affirmation <u>in</u> God as to what the heart has already heard and resolved to believe from the Holy Spirit.

Let's consider how Jesus prayed. First, we know that He prayed without ceasing in that He heard the Father's promptings at all times in all places (Jn. 5:19, 30; 8:28-29, 38; 12:49-50; 14:10). Jesus' conversations with His Father were all internal heart dialogues. Jesus went out of His way to make sure to inform all around Him that He did not need to orally speak <u>to</u> or orally hear <u>from</u> His Heavenly Father (Jn. 11:41-42; 12:27-30). Jesus prayed out loud for the benefit of others, and not for the benefit of Himself. Jesus <u>already</u> knew from His heart interactions with the Father what, when and how the works of God would manifest.

Even in Gethsemane, Jesus wanted the disciples to stay awake so that they could hear and later record that prayer for <u>our</u> benefit. Jesus did not need to <u>orally</u> confer with the Godhead because He had learned to heart-listen for the Father at all times. While the Father did speak at Jesus' baptism, there was no indication He was responding to some specific prayer request by Jesus. Instead, the Father was most likely speaking for the benefit of <u>others</u> present to confirm that Jesus was the Messiah. **"And lo a voice from heaven, saying, This is my beloved Son, in whom I am well pleased."** Matt. 3:17. Most assuredly, Jesus already knew He was the beloved Son of God and that the Father was well pleased.

Think about it. We never hear the Father verbally respond to Jesus' oral prayers recorded elsewhere in Scripture, except in John 12:28-30. Yet here Jesus clearly tells all that the voice of the Father was for their benefit and not His. And in fact, Jesus tells us in John 11:42 that His own oral prayer was not for the benefit of the Father or Himself, but rather was for the benefit of those nearby that they would know Jesus was from God. Jesus then ordered Lazarus back to life. And Lazarus obeyed. Death obeyed. Resurrection manifested.

This leads us to the greatest revelation of prayer Jesus ever taught. In Luke 11 and Matthew 6 Jesus recites the Lord's Prayer and instructs the disciples to "pray this <u>way</u>." Greek scholars agree that Jesus spoke the Lord's Prayer in the imperative mood. As discussed previously, there are four basic moods in the Greek language - - subjective, optative, indicative and imperative. The mood itself refers to the attitude of the speaker toward the verb he is using. The subjective mood basically has the speaker believing what he says (or prays) "might" happen <u>if</u> certain other conditions occur. The optative mood has the speaker "hope" that what he says (or prays) may happen. The indicative mood has the speaker say (or pray) what the current situation "appears" to be to him. Jesus didn't pray in these three moods. He didn't pray that the Kingdom of God "might" come. Nor did Jesus pray that the Kingdom of God would "hopefully" come. Nor did Jesus pray based on factual appearances that the Kingdom of God "needs" to come. (See John 7:24).

Jesus prayed the Lord's Prayer in the imperative mood. Kingdom come! This is the mood of command and authority.

"For I have not spoken of myself; but the Father which sent me, he gave me a commandment, what I should say, and what I should speak. And I know that his commandment is life everlasting: whatsoever I speak therefore, even as the Father said unto me, so I speak." Jn. 12:49-50.

He wasn't asking, begging, wishing or opining that the Father send His Kingdom to Earth. Jesus was ordering His surrounding reality to conform to His Father's Kingdom. He wasn't speaking <u>to</u> reach God the Father. He was speaking <u>from</u> having already embraced God the Father. Jesus had already conferred with God the Father through abiding heart-prayer. His verbal prayer was the external expression of a matter already internally resolved and concluded.

Most, if not all of us, have been taught to pray in any mood <u>but</u> the imperative. This is why there is so much failure and lack of spiritual power. We do not pray "this way," the way of Jesus, the way of the imperative. We beg or wish <u>at</u> God rather than issuing orders <u>from</u> and <u>through</u> God. Paul Billheimer rightly said, "Prayer is not overcoming reluctance in God. It is implementing His decision. It is enforcing His will upon the Earth." Thus, prayer is not about overcoming reluctance in God, but rather overcoming reluctance in us - - reluctance to believe God for all things.

This same dynamic occurs when the Scriptures instruct us "ask in Jesus' name." Let's again consider John 15:7: **"If ye abide in me, and my words abide in you, ye shall ask what ye will, and it shall be done unto you."** Beloved, is this not exactly the issue? First we abide in relational heart-prayer with God. <u>Then</u> we "ask" out loud and it shall be done. This is the imperative faith that comes only from abiding <u>in</u> Christ.

Do you see? Praying in the imperative is the same thing as asking in Jesus' name. We are not begging, wishing, seeking or inquiring with our verbal prayers. We are commanding <u>our</u> immediate sphere of influence to come under the dominion of God's goodness. As an example, when David prayed Psalm 103:1-5, he was <u>commanding</u> his own soul to conform to the dominion and goodness of God. **"Bless the LORD, O my soul: and all that is within me, bless his holy name. Bless the LORD, O my soul, and forget not all his benefits: Who forgiveth all thine iniquities; who healeth all thy diseases; Who redeemeth thy life from destruction; who crowneth thee with lovingkindness and tender mercies; Who satisfieth thy mouth with good things; so that thy youth is renewed like the eagle's."** Ps. 103:1-5.

Again, it's not that we are telling the Father what to do. Rather, it is that we have in our hearts already heard and resolved ourselves to the Holy Spirit's promptings. Our verbal prayer is the exclamation point that completes the circuit of God abiding <u>within</u> us to God manifesting <u>out</u> of us. According to an early Aramaic translation of Genesis 2:7, God created us to be "speaking spirits." When we are abiding in the Holy Ghost, which should and can be 24/7, we are anointed to speak the imperative will of God into this earthly realm as it already is in Heaven. Interlinear translations of Matthew 16:19 agree that Jesus tells Peter that, "Whatever you bind or loose on Earth shall occur, having <u>already</u> been bound or loosed in Heaven." The keys of the Kingdom referred to here were the realization and recognition of imperative prayer as perfect speech. Jesus <u>spoke</u> differently than all the scribes because He spoke with imperative authority. His listeners were astonished at the difference (Mk. 1:22).

Prayer is perfect speech because it amens and affirms the "always already" completed work of the Cross. Verbal prayers don't initiate the power of God. They punctuate it. The roots of true prayer grow deep, wide and strong in the heart-soil of men. Only those with a healthy root system of continual abiding in the Holy Spirit are able to effectively launch the verbal missiles of imperative prayer. **"If any man speak, let him speak as the oracles of God; if any man minister, let him do it as of the ability which God giveth: that God in all things may be glorified through Jesus Christ, to whom be praise and dominion for ever and ever. Amen."** 1 Pet. 4:11.

Quench Not the Spirit

Want to hear the "always already" will of God? Here it is: **"Rejoice evermore. Pray without ceasing. In every thing give thanks: for this is the will of God in Christ Jesus concerning you. Quench not the Spirit."** 1 Thes. 5:16-19. Let me put it another way. God's will <u>in</u> Christ Jesus for you is to rejoice evermore, pray without ceasing and in everything give thanks - - anything short of this <u>quenches</u> the Holy Spirit. This incredible passage can only be fulfilled for those who accept the "always already" Kingdom of God. We can only rejoice "evermore" if evil has been vanquished for "evermore." We can only pray without ceasing if the gift of God has rendered us <u>capable</u> of non-stop intimacy with the Lord. We can only give thanks in everything if God's completed victory encompasses everything. **"These things I have spoken unto you, that in me ye might have peace. In the world ye shall have tribulation: but be of good cheer; I <u>have</u> (already) overcome the world."** Jn. 16:33.

The Holy Spirit convinces us in our heart of these great truths. When our heart listens, the Holy Spirit is empowered to strengthen our souls. When our heart doesn't listen (i.e. neglects our so great a salvation) then the Spirit is quenched and our souls harden to the presence of God.

The Holy Spirit is a friend who sticks closer than a brother.

If we train our heart to look to, listen for and lean on the Holy Spirit at all times, then we can fulfill 1 Thes. 5:16-19. As I was writing this very paragraph, I noticed that the word "heart" has the word "hear" imbedded in it. I then noticed that "t" in heart resembled the Cross. The meaning was astounding - - the heart is the part of us that can "hear" the "t" (Cross). To hear the Cross is to perceive the past completed work of Christ and how it has specifically provided us salvation in our current situations.

Jesus promised us that the Holy Spirit was the gift of God who would "not speak of Himself; but whatsoever He shall hear; that shall He speak: and shall shew it unto you. All things the Father hath are mine: therefore, said I, that He shall take of mine, and shall shew it unto you." Jn. 16:13-15. Praise God, the Holy Spirit "hears" only Jesus. Praise God, the Holy Spirit "speaks" only what He hears. Praise God, the Holy Spirit "shows us" what He hears by speaking it to our hearts. Finally, Praise God, if we heart-listen to "what saith the Spirit," then the faith of Jesus, the nature of Jesus and the fullness of the Father's blessing on Jesus will manifest up, through and out of us. This is the Rhema Word.

To not heart-listen to the Holy Spirit quenches Him. Just as water quenches the warmth and light of a campfire, neglecting the inner fire of the Spirit quenches its light and warmth for your soul. While the fire of God's Spirit can be quenched by a hardened heart, it can never be fully extinguished. A hearing heart oxygenates the Spirit to burn more and more brightly in your soul. A hardened and neglectful heart diminishes and douses the Spirit's fire in your soul. Smith Wigglesworth said, *"If you want to increase in the life of God, then you must settle it in your heart that you will not at any time resist the Holy*

Spirit. The Holy Spirit and fire - - the fire burning up every-
thing that would impoverish and destroy you."

I love how the first Christians prioritized the Holy Spirit. Their
attitude for every decision was, "It seems good to the Holy
Spirit <u>and</u> us" (Acts 15:28). They put the promptings of the
Spirit first, even before their own opinions. And so can we.
The yoke of the Spirit is light and not burdensome. The sons
of God are those led by the Spirit of God - - and led, and led,
and led (Rom. 8:14). Don't make this a heavy burden. It's not
about you. It's about God. Don't beat yourself up because you
haven't heart-listened like you should have in the past. The
point is you can start listening <u>now</u>. God promises whoever
listens <u>will</u> hear. The Spirit is <u>always</u> speaking to your heart.
Trust this. Ignore any other option. You <u>can</u> hear God. The
Word is near you - - in your heart and mouth (Rom. 10:8).

Parable of Prayer

Once there was a young and earnest beggar who found a
huge rock of "fool's gold" in the riverbed. He thought it was
real gold and valuable beyond calculation. He confidently
strode into town showing off his new fortune - - the solution
to all his wants. He took the rock to the kind and gener-
ous merchant jeweler who dealt in all precious commodities.
The jeweler immediately knew the rock was fool's gold and
was worthless. Yet, the jeweler saw that it would crush the
spirit of the boy to expose his monumental mistake. Instead,
the jeweler convinced the boy to allow him to store the rock
in his own safe. Then the jeweler convinced the beggar to
come to work for him for a few months so that he could
learn how best to value and handle the riches his rock would
surely bring when it was sold. The beggar worked for the

wise jeweler and grew steadily in wisdom and knowledge. The boy began to realize for himself that the rock in the safe was fool's gold because of his daily exposure to the "true" gold the jeweler dealt in. The boy realized and appreciated the merchant's tender mercy in trying to help correct him without crushing him. The boy saw that the merchant enabled him to learn truth in an environment of love, nurture and freedom. The boy stayed working with the jeweler in absolute obedience and trust for the rest of his days. He became his son. He became his heir.

Beloved, I know that the Lord teaches us the same way. Many of us have <u>never</u> prayed in the imperative mood because we thought ourselves beggars before God. We have adopted methods of begging or wishing prayer that we thought were precious gold. The Lord took all our previous prayers without chastising or breaking our spirits and locked them in His safe. Meanwhile, He has gradually developed our senses to discern the true gold of imperative prayer. Like the beggar, we all will realize for ourselves what true gold is. This means we will come to understand why our fool's gold never brought us success. But, hallelujah, in this process we have discovered the love and goodness of the Father who patiently endures our errors and leads us to the true riches found only in His Son Jesus Christ.

The "You" Adjustment

Let me show you an adjustment which will help stop your verbal prayers from being little more than begging, wishing or complaining sessions. My two favorite Psalms are 51 and 91. Psalm 51 is the best prayer of repentance ever written. Psalm 91 is the best imperative prayer of deliverance and protection ever written. Psalm 91 doesn't need an adjustment. It perfectly reveals authoritative and imperative commands of safety, preservation, healing, deliverance, angelic protection and complete victory. On the other hand, Psalm 51 needs a slight New Testament mood adjustment.

For instance, instead of verbally asking the Lord to blot out our transgressions or begging Him to create in us a new heart or wishing that He would renew a steadfast spirit within us; what if instead, after our hearts had already interacted with the Holy Spirit over these issues, we then ordered ourselves to receive God's benefits of forgiveness in the form of a command. "Lord, **You** create in me a new heart! **You** renew a steadfast spirit in me! Lord, **You** blot out my transgressions!" See the difference? Under the imperative reading, there is no room for doubt, failure, wishing or begging. Our mood of command comes from being already convinced in our heart by the Holy Spirit's witness that God's nature is to forgive all our sins. Inserting "**You**" at the front end of prayers sets the imperative mood. Jesus didn't say, "Please hear me Father." Jesus said, "I thank **You** Father that **You** always hear me." Jn. 11:41-42 paraphrase. Jesus didn't pray at His time of greatest need, "Father, please don't leave my soul in Hell and please don't let me see corruption." Jesus prayed, "**You** will not leave my soul in Hell or allow me to see corruption." Acts 2:27, 31 paraphrase.

Remember Chapter One? If a home intruder were attacking my children, they wouldn't yell "Dad, would you please help us?" They would yell "Dad, help!" This is because they know my nature must help them. They are in effect ordering my help because of their confidence in my character and love. How can we do any less with God? This was the key to the Roman Centurion's faith, which Jesus said was greater than any He had seen in Israel - - the Centurion recognized that greater authority <u>always</u> speaks in the imperative and <u>always</u> must be obeyed (Matt. 8:5-13).

As long as I verbally ask in any mood other than the imperative, then I remain unconvinced and have handcuffed the power of God from being released through my confession. Praying in the imperative keeps the focus on God and not me. Sure, we need to repent on a daily basis, but repentance is a work of the heart and the Holy Ghost. It is not a work of asking God and waiting on an answer that He may or may not forgive me - - someday, somehow, maybe yes, maybe no. Beloved, God is greater than our hearts - - always greater, more available, more accessible than any of us realize. Once the Holy Spirit reveals God's goodness to you, you can never beg Him again. It's His good pleasure to give you His Kingdom of forgiveness, healing and salvation. Always His good pleasure. The imperative mood is the key to perfect speech, perfect praise, perfect thanksgiving, perfect patience and perfect faith. Perfection comes by imperative speaking. Imperative speaking comes by faith. Faith comes by hearing. Hearing comes by the Rhema Word of God. The Rhema Word comes by paying our tithe of attention to the *idea\seed\ Logos* of God. This is the way God's Word is performed in this realm.

As stated in the previous chapter, the word "perform" means "to carry out or execute an action or process." To perform Scripture is the Word becoming flesh in us. Just as great actors internalize their characters' true nature based on the playwright's script, so do we internalize Jesus' divine nature in us by meditating on the Scriptures. The Scriptures "inform" us of the true nature of God, but the Holy Spirit in us "performs" this truth unto manifestation until we become "doers" (actors) of the Word (Jas. 1:22-26). Just as actors rehearse their roles until they become one with the character, so do we rehearse righteousness until the Word becomes flesh in us.

We don't memorize, confess and rehearse Scriptures so that we can give "mechanical" recitations. No, we memorize, confess and rehearse Scriptures so that the nature of God will percolate and brew within us - - the very nature and power and goodness of our God. Then, we will overflow as manifest sons of God. This is the mood that then allows us to rejoice evermore and in everything give thanks. True worship and thanksgiving flow fervently and automatically when we see God's promises are "always already" fulfilled and completed in Christ.

Jesus has left nothing undone, no enemy undefeated and no promise unfulfilled. When we stop neglecting this truth, we will start truly believing it. Stopping the neglect of God's so great a salvation is what *The Jesus Mood* is all about.

The Jesus Mood is about the *Tree of Life* <u>inside</u> us - - Christ <u>in</u> us the hope of glory (Col. 1:27)! Because the Logos of life is planted in the center of our being, we can receive and release the imperative Rhemas of God. These Rhemas command life and reconcile reality back to the will of God. It's all about certainty. Certainty, certainty, certainty. <u>Only</u> the *Tree of Life* provides the reality and certainty of *The Jesus Mood*. May this book help provide you a <u>refining</u> tool to help you incarnate the big idea planted into you when you were born again. This big idea may have been dormant, but now it's time to live and grow into *The Jesus Mood*. Beloved, the mind, mood and motive of Jesus all are planted firmly inside you. Start paying your tithe of attention to this idea, and it will grow and grow until the reality of it dwarfs every other thing in your life. Then the works of God will manifest. The life of God will manifest. And you too will manifest as a beloved son of God.

Apokalypsis

There once was a land of white sheets and dark shapes,
The horrors of Hell the sheets did well drape.

For if any did see the true state of things,
Madness would follow, then death with its sting.

Yet the vague shapes that remained could still chill to the bone,
The sense of what lay beneath turned the heart into stone.

All men greatly feared what the sheets did conceal,
For embedded beneath the world's fallen nature was revealed.

So God in His mercy allowed the sheets to remain,
Fig leaves behind which men could hide shame.

But God had a plan to renovate His creation,
Newness would come to every kindred and nation.

At the Cross, the blessed Son suffered stroke after stroke,
So that His love could penetrate through each and every cloak.

Each sheet was injected with the shed blood of Christ,
The evil beneath was cured by this sweet sacrifice.

The sheets still remained to husk all we see,
But now beneath them all beat drums of victory.

So when you see a sheet of appearance with the outline of doom,
Don't be deceived, use your faith to rebuke all gloom.

Everything has been put under the foot of our Lord,
Above, beneath and between, all submitted to His sword.

All things are subject to Him and must bend their knee,
For long ago He did disarm every enemy.

Captivity is captive, all slaves have been freed,
Neglect not your salvation in word, thought or deed.

So disrobe all appearances of their sheets of distress,
God's total salvation will now manifest.

Start looking at these sheets as a way to unveil,
A living statute of Jesus as the head and not the tail.

As we stop the neglect of this always great fact,
We will rip off the sheets with great confidence and tact.

Some sheets we can yank off with the power of one,
But other bigger sheets may take the teamwork of sons.

What remains to be seen will be seen and remain,
The world is always already reconciled to His name.

About the Author

Richard K. Murray is a practicing attorney from Dalton, Georgia where he lives with his wife Rita and their seven children: Sloan, Caleb, Micah, Abraham, Sarah, Ben and Annie. Richard has a B.B.A. and J.D. from the University of Georgia and a M.A. from Regent University School of Divinity. He has written several books, including *Rouse the Mighty Men, The New Covenant, Voyaging Through God's Goodness, The Spiritual Eye of the Tiger, The Power* and *Lift Up Your Jawbone.*

Contact at 200-A West Gordon Street, Dalton, Georgia 30720, (706)272-3289, or visit www.thegoodnessofgod.com.

LaVergne, TN USA
14 September 2009
157762LV00001B/1/P